10-4-65

MISSION
MYTH *and*
REALITY

9

MISSION

MYTH *and*

REALITY

Keith Bridston

FRIENDSHIP PRESS   *New York*

First printing June 1965
Second printing August 1965

LIBRARY OF CONGRESS CATALOG
CARD NUMBER: 65-11426

*To Kenneth Scott Latourette
and W. A. Visser 't Hooft
and to my students in Indonesia
and America*

CONTENTS

INTRODUCTION

This book is autobiographical. Although the style may not suggest that fact, the following pages are a self-history. They are a chronicle, in reflective form, of one man's intellectual and spiritual struggle with the meaning of the Christian mission.

It is difficult to know where this struggle began. When and how are the primal concepts of the mission of the church communicated? Certainly it is not only through formal educational channels and media. A great deal of what is thought about mission is simply absorbed, osmotically, when one is in the church. In fact, many of the most important elements are never articulated at all. Not infrequently these are in contradiction to the stated theories and principles the churches proclaim and teach. And it is often these deep-seated, subconscious assumptions rather than formal policies that determine the nature of the missionary enterprise.

The term "myth" is intended to point to that ambivalence. Robert Graves and Raphael Patai in *Hebrew Myths* define myths as "dramatic stories that form a sacred charter either authorizing the continuance of ancient institutions, customs, rites and beliefs in the area where they are current, or approving alterations." The missionary movement developed its own mythology. It is the thesis of this book that until that mythology is recognized and critically analyzed, efforts either to reform the enterprise or to give it a new rationale are premature. The roots of motivation and action are untouched by such superficial approaches. Reform is always possible. But around what central orienting principle? Throwing out one old, anachronistic form of mission may result in its replacement by seven worse ones.

Bishop J. E. Lesslie Newbigin speaks to this point: "How very much of our failure in missionary work is due to the failure to distinguish between that which is essential in the visible form of the Church and that which is merely a thing that our fathers and grandfathers were brought up in!"[1] What criterion, or criteria, can be used to make such distinctions? The fact is that the mythology determines our judgments on such matters. We seek to be rational and scientific in distinguishing the essential from the nonessential. Crucial points, however, escape scrutiny because they are subrational and mythologically determined.

Many approaches to the study of missions remind one of the studies of the human personality before the

Notes will be found on page 125.

time of Freud, or the analyses of social and political life before the time of Marx. The seven-eighths submerged portion of the "iceberg"—the dark mythological mass that gives buoyancy to the one-eighth section floating above—is left untouched.

At this stage, however, the mythological substratum defies exact and precise rational analysis or description. In a sense, it can only be pointed to and its importance emphasized. It is something to be aware of and, in some ways, beware of. Herbert Butterfield in *The Origins of Modern Science* shows how the dead weight of old presuppositions hinders intellectual advance; Aristotelian physics, for example, was a hindrance not simply because it was venerable but also because it was part of a system that was such a colossal intellectual feat in itself that it was hard to free the human mind of its presuppositions. But until the old system was abandoned, nothing new could take its place.

"Myth" is used here in this general sense. James Barr of Princeton says that "Myth is then a total world outlook: not an outlook brought to expression only on certain solemn occasions, rather one which informs and inspires with meaning the daily business of living." To scrutinize the mythological *weltanschauung* underlying the missionary enterprise is more threatening to its defenders and apologists than to criticize its external forms or stated policies, because the core of its dynamic is put under radical questioning. It is also more frustrating because a rigorous demythologizing of missions

11

does not easily or quickly lead to a positive theoretical or programmatic reconstruction. "Be positive" is easier to say than to do. As Butterfield writes of the scientific revolution in the seventeenth century:

While everything was in the melting-pot—the older order undermined but the new scientific system unachieved—the conflict was bitterly exasperated, men actually calling for a revolution, not merely for an explanation of existing anomalies but for a new science and a new method . . . it is clear that some men were highly conscious of the predicament in which the world now found itself. They seemed to be curiously lacking in discernment in one way, however, for they tended to believe that the scientific revolution could be carried out entirely in a single lifetime. It was a case of changing one lantern-slide of the universe for another, in their opinion—establishing a new system to take the place of Aristotle's. Gradually they found that it would need not merely one generation but perhaps two to complete the task.[2]

The rise of the ecumenical movement has this Copernican character in relation to the missionary task. The problem of defining a new view of mission is not simply that of recasting the old, familiar elements in a new pattern. Revolution rather than reform is the appropriate term to describe what has happened in the last half century. If the nineteenth century was the "Great Century" of Christian expansion, the latter half of the twentieth century is the dawn of a new "Ecumenical Era." It may prove to be as radical in its implications for the missionary outlook of the Christian church as the Copernican revolution was for the scientific cosmology of its day.

As has been said, this book is the record of one man's personal pilgrimage along the missionary way during this period of revolutionary transition in the church's view of its nature and task in the world. As an undergraduate at Yale, I was a member of the Student Volunteer Movement. I think I can understand something of the austere challenge of the traditional call to foreign missions and the invigorating demands it placed on personal commitment and the sacrificial spirit of self-giving for a great cause. Prevented by political upheaval from going to China as a Yale-in-China bachelor—a prototype of contemporary Peace Corps service—I went to Scotland as a chaplain to overseas students in Edinburgh under the auspices of the Student Christian Movement in Great Britain and Ireland. Working in this cosmopolitan educational center for two and a half years gave an unparalleled opportunity to meet and mix with the new "elite" from the emerging independent countries of Africa, Asia, and Central and South America and to experience through them the tremendous conflict and stimulation that the confrontation between Western and non-Western cultures has brought about in our day.

Three and a half years on the staff of the World's Student Christian Federation in Geneva followed. This meant a total immersion in ecumenical affairs at one of the most critical periods in recent ecumenical history—the post-Amsterdam era of the formation of the

World Council of Churches. It also meant the opportunity of traveling and seeing the classic mission fields. The dialectical interpenetration of unity and mission was an existential constant for anyone working in a Geneva ecumenical office from 1948 to 1952.

A phone call from J. C. Hoekendijk, then Secretary for Evangelism of the WCC, one summer morning in 1952 made the missionary call concrete: Would I go to Indonesia to teach at the Higher Theological College in Djakarta? Just packing for a trip when the phone rang, I had five minutes to decide. The answer was "Yes." Two months later we were landing at the Kemajaran Airport—living examples of ecumenical partnership in mission, for our salary was provided by the Presbyterian Board of Foreign Missions in the U.S.A., the invitation was communicated to us and our travel paid by the Dutch Reformed Board of Missions at Oegstgeest, and we were serving in an Indonesian institution—and we were Lutherans!

After a year in Djakarta, a call from the Council of the Batak Church in Sumatra to be a professor of theology in their new Universitas Nommensen, in process of formation, led us to Pematang Siantar, supported by the Lutheran World Federation as part of its world mission program. The years in Indonesia—turbulent, exciting, distressing, exhilarating, and supremely stimulating—gave us a uniquely precious opportunity to live through the revolution in missions microcosmically. The lessons to be learned from the history of the Christian community there, especially in the years of revolution from 1945 to the present, are only beginning to be understood and are certainly not yet fully digested. One might say that if the Christian churches' history in Indonesia *and* China, especially since World War II, could be properly appreciated and appropriated, that would be all the textbook needed for preparing to enter the new ecumenical era of mission.

In 1957 another call to Geneva, this time to be a staff member of the World Council of Churches with special responsibility for Faith and Order work, meant reentering the atmosphere of ecumenical bureaucracy. The four years that followed were focused on the particular theological and institutional problems of Christian unity as articulated in the program of the Commission on Faith and Order. The dialectical polarity of unity and mission was again vividly evident, especially in the negotiations leading to the integration of the WCC and the International Missionary Council in 1961.

Fifteen years after embarking from New York for Europe, we returned to the United States—having completed a much longer overseas voyage then we had anticipated. But those fifteen years also, if they could be fully appreciated and appropriated, could have much to say about the dawning ecumenical era of mission. This book attempts, in a somewhat poetic and indirect way, to be a mirror for that experience.

The speculations that follow are not based primarily on theory, but on a commitment to the Christian mission and on an actual involvement in it in many different places. Out of this varied experience has come the conviction that a reformation of the missionary movement is not enough. The changing global environment as well as the theological revolution, which has required radical shifts of perspective in many fields—the "new hermeneutic" connected with the Bultmannite movement and related to contemporary secular existentialism, the Christological restructuring of dogmatics by Barth, and the ecclesiological reappraisal ushered in by the ecumenical movement, to mention only some examples—suggest that a profound transformation is demanded. That transformation involves not simply the missionary movement as a semi-autonomous entity within or beside the church, but a radical new view of the church itself as an institutional organism and earthly community being *the* mission.

The implications of this new view are only beginning to dawn on us. In a negative way, it can be seen that the old forms of mission, for example, foreign missions, may be largely finished. The organizational expressions and institutional embodiments of the Christian mission known as missions or the missionary movement are like fruit on a tree whose roots have been torn loose by a storm; the tree continues to bear, but in a residual rather than a dynamic way. The judgment of death is upon it. Its potential life rests not in itself but in the seeds, which must be buried and resurrected —transformed into new beings.

As Father Albert J. Nevins, editor of *Maryknoll* magazine, told the fifteenth annual meeting of American Catholic mission societies, "the missionary era as we have known it is gone and will never return." Those who fail to recognize this fact are doomed to be "as contemporary as a dodo bird." His conclusion: "Change and you can survive; fail to change and your effectiveness is ended."[3]

The idea that a reformation of missions would be an adequate change fails to take into account the possibility that the traditional forms of mission are themselves irreformable because they embody a response to a world that no longer exists and express a theological understanding of the relation of the world to God that is now felt to be fallacious. The mission response expressed by traditional missions is not negated, but the essential form of that response is. The implication of modification and basic continuity of the traditional forms of mission carried by the term "reformation" excludes the more revolutionary possibilities of transformation, that is, the possibilities of death and resurrection. When the practical implications of this are worked out, the reasons why reformation rather than transformation is the more appealing way are not difficult to discern. To suggest, for example, that the vocational category of "missionary," or more especially "foreign missionary," is in practice irrelevant and theologically unjustified and that it is a form of mission that may have to die puts the livelihood of a great number of persons in jeopardy. Industrial workers are similarly threatened by the transformation of factory production through automation brought on by the technological revolution.

In neither case is the solution easy, but in neither case does a viable solution mean turning the clocks back or stopping them. Or to suggest that the form of mission incorporated in mission boards is sociologically anachronistic and ecclesiologically questionable and that transformation rather than reformation is required poses a considerable psychological threat to those who are most directly connected with such bodies. It also poses equally difficult organizational problems in working out the practical ramifications of transforming a corporate entity whose annual budget may be, in the case of one American foreign mission board, more than $30,000,000. Reformation involving relatively moderate change *may* be the solution, but there is no guarantee that it will be. The point is that the magnitude of the changes in our time *may* require radical transformation, in short, the actual death of the old forms, in order that the church may fulfill its mission today and tomorrow. That possibility cannot be excluded in any realistic appraisal of the mission of the church in the contemporary world, however threatening such an appraisal may be.

The purpose of this book is to raise such questions. If herein solutions are less evident, this fact is simply an accurate reflection of the situation we find ourselves in at present. For until the right questions are asked, the right answers are not likely to be uncovered. It is the author's belief that we are still at the first stage— of discovering the right questions—in considering the nature and form of the Christian mission today.

For that reason, the spirit of this book is radical. It is also critical, but the criticisms are intended to get at the right questions and are therefore intended to be constructive rather than destructive. Such critical probing may be painful, but it is a necessary precondition for accurate diagnosis, and eventual curative prescriptions depend upon it. The author suspects that the problem in missions today is not one or two or three cases of institutional malfunctioning for which reformation would be the appropriate correction, but a situation in which the traditional forms of mission, and more particularly foreign missions, are basically anachronistic. Thus, the only ultimately effective solution is radical transformation of the whole life of the church. To pursue the scientific analogy again, as can now be seen in the discovery of the circulation of the blood by Harvey, the barrier to the break-through was a complex system of errors concerning which it has to be noted that the doctrine was not only wrong in itself, but, until it was put right, it stood as a permanent barrier against . . . advance, for, indeed, nothing else could be right. It is another of those cases in which we can say that once this matter was rectified the way lay open to a tremendous flood of further changes elsewhere."[4] The mythology of missions is just such a complex system of errors, a barrier to advance and further change in the mission of the church. Because this mythology has been very pervasive and, as is generally true, very subtle and difficult to detect, examination of the right questions has been excluded by concentration on the questions of missions. As Martin Werner notes in describing the development of Christian doctrine:

This entanglement in problems, which were misconceived, throws into strong relief the failure of ancient Catholicism relative to the real problems. . . . Thus perhaps in this context also the reassuring words of the philosopher Emil Utilz will be proved true: "Often the way to the right question is longer and more thorny than the way to the right solution."

The thesis of this book is that the real question is: *whose* mission? And related to this basic one are the following: *where* mission? *what* mission? *how* mission? *by whom* mission? The chapters are meant to pose these questions. The conclusion is to suggest how the answer to these questions may precisely involve the transformation that has been mentioned. Perhaps one of the most remarkable facts about the ecumenical movement is that it has, apparently, been giving answers to questions that the church far too long has failed to ask.

—KEITH R. BRIDSTON

1 THE GEOGRAPHICAL MYTH AND THE ONENESS OF THE CHURCH

Out to sea. The sea—which was pure, safe, and friendly. . . . The sea was now the only remedy for all my troubles.

Joseph Conrad

WATER! WHAT CHORDS IT STRIKES IN THE HUMAN SPIRIT. What visions it conjures in the human mind. What power it exerts on the human will. For those who eke out their existence on the parched desert, it is life. For those who dwell on the edge of the sea, it is life as well. With water—and word—man can live.

Bodies of water! What challenges they raise for land-bound man. What mysteries they suggest in their limitless horizons. From the sea man has come, and to the sea he must return. In some dim way he remembers the water as his primordial home and, fearsome as it may be, he must launch out upon the restless waves to find himself. As Herman Melville begins in *Moby Dick:*

If they but knew it, almost all men in their degree, some time or other, cherish very nearly the same feelings towards the ocean with me. . . . Circumambulate the city on a dreamy Sabbath afternoon. Go from Corlears Hok to Coenties Slip, and from thence, by Whitehall, northward. What do you see?—Posted like silent sentinels all around the town, stand thousands upon thousands of mortal men fixed in ocean reveries. . . . They must get just as nigh the water as they possibly can without falling in. And there they stand—miles of them—leagues. Inlanders all, they come from lanes and alleys, streets and avenues—north, east, south, and west. Yet here they all unite. . . .

Once more. Say, you are in the country; in some high land of lakes. Take almost any path you please, and ten to one it carries you down in a dale, and leaves you there by a pool in the stream. There is magic in it. Let the most absent-minded of men be plunged in his deepest reveries— stand that man on his legs, set his feet a-going, and he will infallibly lead you to water, if water there be in all that region. . . . Yes, as every one knows, meditation and water are wedded for ever. . . . Why did the old Persians hold the sea holy? Why did the Greeks give it a separate deity, and own brother of Jove? Surely all this is not without meaning. And still deeper the meaning of that story of Narcissus, who because he could not grasp the tormenting, mild image he saw in the fountain, plunged into it and was drowned. But that same image, we ourselves see in all rivers and oceans. It is the image of the ungraspable phantom of life; and this is the key to it all.

Man is an incurable voyager. Whether it is the walls of his hut, the circle of his village, the ridge of the next hill, or the vast sweep of the limitless sea—he must be out and away. No demons can deter him, no threats can prevent him, no dangers can divert him from going. He must, and he does.

It is not surprising that the greatest of all physical bodies in man's world, the oceans, should be his archetypal frontier. They symbolize the unknown that man must challenge—or die. And even today those immense bodies remain untamed by man and, to a surprising degree in a scientific age, mysterious and unknown.

So the symbol remains vital and powerful. Man, the roamer, becomes a foreign missionary. He is mobile and the sea is before him. Those who have gone before and come back—even those who have not come back—tantalize him with the irresistible attraction of the foreign shore. Listen to one of those foreign sailors:

And this is how I see the East. I have seen its secret places and have looked into its very soul; but now I see it always from a small boat, a high outline of mountains, blue and afar in the morning; like faint mist at noon; a jagged wall of purple at sunset. I have the feel of the oar in my hand, the vision of a scorching blue sea in my eyes. And I see a bay, a wide bay, smooth as glass and polished like ice, shimmering in the dark. A red light burns far off upon the gloom of the land, and the night is soft and warm. We drag at the oars with aching arms, and suddenly a puff of

wind, a puff faint and tepid and laden with strange odours
of blossoms, of aromatic wood, comes out of the still night—
the first sigh of the East on my face. That I can never forget. It was impalpable and enslaving, like a charm, like a
whispered promise of mysterious delight. . . . A current rip-
pled softly. The scented obscurity of the shore was grouped
into vast masses, a density of colossal clumps of vegetation,
probably—mute and fantastic shapes. And at their foot the
semicircle of a beach gleamed faintly, like an illusion. There
was not a light, not a stir, not a sound. The mysterious East
faced me, perfumed like a flower, silent like death, dark
like a grave. And I sat weary beyond expression, exulting
like a conqueror, sleepless and entranced as if before a
profound, a fateful enigma.[1]

There have been many explanations for the Christian
foreign missionary enterprise. Missionary literature
bulges with them. Admitting the multiplicity of factors involved, one of the most significant—and one seldom considered—is the coincidence of religious passion and romantic appeal. Christians, we are told, went
out because they were commanded to preach the gospel to the ends of the earth. But perhaps they would
have gone out anyway: They were, after all, only human and, in that also, missionary.

The combination of the two elements, the theological and the anthropological, was what made it fission-
able, explosive, expansive. Water and word—together
they cover and conquer the world. The baptismal flood
and fire will not be contained. The conflagrational wave
sweeps forward. Kenneth Scott Latourette points out:

Never has the world seen anything quite to equal it. Not only has the record never been approached by any religion . . . but never before in the history of the race has any group of ideas, religious, social, economic, or political, been propagated over so wide an area or among so many people by so many who have given their lives to the task.

Historical events of this magnitude are not easily explainable. Indeed, they may ultimately be unexplainable, so closely are they interwoven with the unfathomable mysteries of man's own nature and destiny and God's cosmic design. Insofar, however, as they are able to be empirically analyzed, it is evident that the expansion of Europe and the expansion of Christianity coinhere. Even before the end of the Middle Ages this was true: "The Crusades, in reality the first of those imperialistic ventures that Europe has sent out to despoil and appropriate the earth, soon came to be as much commercial as religious enterprises."[2] The Italians, who had prospered both from transporting crusaders and from trading with their enemies, were by the thirteenth century in regular connection with commercial centers of the East—the Levant, India, Russia, China. The Venetian Marco Polo aroused interest in the exotic realms of the Far East, and as the Portuguese and the Spaniards joined in the movement outwards to share in the wealthy trade of the Italian ports, little by little the naive provincialism of medieval Europe gave way to a more cosmopolitan outlook. Admittedly, this did not mean "much more than an adolescent interest in the wonders of the earth" for generations and often did not rise much above a "childlike wonder" and not infrequently sank to "the primitive impulse to plunder."

As J. H. Randall points out, neither the Renaissance nor the Reformation was profoundly affected by this widened horizon. Both were essentially the final flower of the Middle Ages rather than first fruits of the new day. Nevertheless, there is among historians a growing recognition of the importance of this enlargement of the geographical horizons of Europe by the discovery of the rest of the world, and the effect of it on the revolutionary changes that came swiftly after 1500. Not least among these was the fact that in numberless ways Europe's expansion forced a direct intellectual reaction on the mind of Christendom. The Christian imagination was stimulated by the vision of great unknown kingdoms, lying open and unclaimed over the edge of the seas. Like Conrad's sailor, the church was "sleepless and entranced as if before a profound, a fateful enigma."

But the entrancement did not break into action immediately. In 1270 Marco Polo communicated an appeal from Kublai Khan to the Pope for a hundred Christian teachers, and this ruler of one of the great empires of all time offered to be baptized along with all the chiefs of China. The response of Rome was two small bands of monks, only six of whom reached their destination. The Christian imagination had obviously not yet been touched by the expanding dimensions of the new geography. It was only when the European

Catholic nations themselves became formally involved in the exploration and exploitation of the new worlds that Roman Catholic missionary efforts flourished.

In some Protestant nations, land-locked or not yet awake to the cosmopolitan era, religious energies were expended for inner organizational consolidation and intellectual formalization. The theological faculty at Wittenberg, asked to give their exegesis of the Great Commission, said: 1. The command "go ye" was meant only for the original apostles. It had already been fulfilled, said the theologians, basing their interpretation on the tradition from the apocraphyl Gospel of St. Thomas that the apostles had remained for fifteen years in Jerusalem and after dividing the world into segments had cast lots to determine who should enter these parts. 2. God had made himself universally known three times in the history of the world: in the times of Adam, Noah, and the apostles. Having had their chance, the heathen had only themselves to blame if they still remained unconverted. 3. It is the duty of the secular authority to see that the gospel is preached—in *its* dominions.

Eric Wahlstrom, in *My Father Worketh Hitherto*, cites a sermon on the Great Commission by a Swedish preacher in 1722, which concluded: "Formerly it was said: Go ye into all the world, but now the command of God to you is: Remain where God has placed you." The venerable Wittenberg doctors were simply reflecting the provincial attitude of church people of the seventeenth and eighteenth centuries. The romantic impact of the new geographical discoveries had, if it

27

had affected their imaginations at all, not penetrated sufficiently to touch their religious or theological sensibilities. The dawning of the implications of the new world being born came in a tangential way to the churches: "It was not until the Enlightenment . . . that Europeans finally realized the magnitude of their world; science and a world-wide cosmopolitanism together ushered in our era."[3]

The subsequent history of the spectacular growth of Protestant missions, reaching its climax in the nineteenth century, need not be repeated here. Just as with the geographical pioneers themselves who were deterred from starting to "confidently set out to girdle this world," whose untouched terrains they suspected, by "two reasons—the dangers of the deep and of strange lands, and the dangers of the greater deep of man's mind" but finally reached "a time when the terrors of the unknown are outweighed by its fascination, when experiment must be tried," so the churches through their missionary pioneers began to overcome their lethargy, and the Christian community's imagination began to be aroused by the new world which was opening up around it.

Count von Zinzendorf's "passion" becomes the distinguishing mark of this new missionary spirit. Suddenly word and water are thrust together in a flaming fusion:

> The whole earth is the Lord's:
> Men's souls are His:
> I am debtor to all.

What fires were ignited by this capturing of the Christian imagination by the thought of preaching the good news to the whole world! It did not, of course, ignite everyone. The English shoemaker, William Carey, was told by the Baptist dignitaries: "Young man, sit down, sit down. You're an enthusiast. When God pleases to convert the heathen, He'll do it without consulting you or me." But divine fire is not quenched, even by ecclesiastical powers. High on a hill in central Sumatra, in 1864, a crippled Danish-German farm boy by the name of Ludwig Nommensen looked over the lush valleys of Batakland, whose fierce cannibalistic inhabitants had violently ended a previous attempt by two young volunteers from the American Board of Commissioners for Foreign Missions in Boston to penetrate their territory, and proclaimed: "Alive or dead, among these folk for whom redemption has been purchased by the precious blood of Christ, I shall remain, O God, and establish your Word and Kingdom." By the time of his death in 1918, the Huria Kristen Batak Protestant (the church he founded) numbered more than 200,000 members!

But not all the stories told of success. From Tabai in East Africa, a widowed missionary wrote in 1844:

Tell our friends at home that there is now on the East African coast a lonely missionary grave. This is a sign that you have commenced the struggle with this part of the world; and as the victories of the Church are gained by stepping over the graves of her members, you may be the more convinced that the hour is at hand when you are summoned to the conversion of Africa from its eastern shore.

29

When the Church Missionary Society was faced with the fact that during the previous year ten out of the twelve recruits sent to West Africa the year before had died, the committee was desperate; but it rallied to the words of a layman: "We must not abandon West Africa." And it didn't.

The storming of the gates of heathendom by such heroic endeavors itself seemed to bring miraculous results. In 1858, often called the "Annus Mirabilis" of missionary history, four great fields were thrown open as never before to missionary penetration—Africa, India, China, and Japan. Livingstone started on his second and most momentous journey into the interior of the "dark continent." The rule of the East India Company, with its antimissionary policy, came to an end in India in 1858 and the Crown assumed authority. With the Treaty of Tientsin, reversing a decree of 1724, China granted religious toleration and the right of Europeans to travel to the inland areas. And in the same year, Japan was opened to foreigners by the Treaty of Yedo, after generations of seclusion.

This dramatic and exotic character of the whole missionary enterprise made it foreign in more than one way to the churches of the West. It was not only far away geographically; it was in many respects alien to their whole way of thought and life. Foreign missions: How could they be much more strange and different? The fact that so much missionary endeavor was initiated and controlled by voluntary, independent missionary societies in the pioneering age reflects the foreign character that missionary work had for the established churches.

Seen from the vantage point of historical detachment, it is understandable why this foreignness of missions came to be misunderstood and misinterpreted —and why these misunderstandings and misinterpretations are only now gradually being corrected. The foreign missionary movement was slowly enveloped in a mythology that eventually almost obscured the realities of its purpose and existence.

For one thing, the amazing success of the nineteenth century missionary enterprise began to be interpreted almost exclusively as the result of an arbitrary, unprecedented intervention of God into human history after apparently nineteen hundred years of withdrawal. The historical confluence of a new geographical awareness and cosmopolitan spirit with a deep current of pietism and evangelicalism was not seen as an empirically verifiable factor in the evolution of the Great Century of missionary expansion. That God can also work spectacularly through such hidden historical channels is not to be denied; but this more subtle and sophisticated appreciation of God's relation to the world and to his people has not been notable in the theology of the missionary movement.

For another thing, the ambivalence of religious and romantic motivations in the calling to be a foreign missionary was not fully appreciated, indeed sometimes not realized at all. The combination of the right ingredients of man's natural adventuresome and experimental spirit, the powerful appeal of the strange and the exotic exposed by the great era of exploration, and pietistic religious passion can be a potent—often explosive—vocational brew. And it was! But, as might have been expected, that power was explained in terms of only one of the ingredients. In fact, the oversimplified religious psychology of pietism, which dominated Protestant action during this period of time, lacked the dimensions to encompass such paradoxical and antithetical motivational factors in explaining Christian vocation, or religious service and action in general. "Woe unto me if I preach not the Gospel" was sufficient explanation—for what St. Paul was and for what the foreign missionary was thought to be, both by the church at home and by himself. He was foreign because the "love of Christ constrained" him to be so. What of the other foreigners he inevitably met in the far corners of the earth? They were there before him, or they came with him, or they followed close behind. They were a reminder of something he could not understand, or wanted to forget.

Finally, it was not just that the mythology surrounding the missionary enterprise obscured the historical forces that formed it and provided its dynamic, or that this mythology camouflaged the mixed motives of those who went out in its name; but this mythology projected the illusion that the primary missionary frontier was geographical. And so developed what might be called the mystical doctrine of salt water. The mission of the church was so closely identified with geographical expansion, and the missionary enterprise so exclusively considered in terms of geographical frontiers, that the term "mission" inevitably had a foreign connotation. Traveling over salt water was thereby gradually changed from being the obvious concomitant of *some* kinds of missionary service, to being the *sine qua non* of *any* kind of missionary endeavor, and finally to being the final test and criterion of what in fact was missionary. Being transported over salt water, the more the better, was given a certain absolute theological and spiritual value.

It would be foolish to suggest that the geographical frontier ever was, or ever will be, insignificant in the missionary activity of the church. But if the religious significance of salt water is seen in any other than a poetic and mythical way, the whole meaning of the mission of the church is in danger of being lost, or so perverted that it would be better lost. The geographical frontier, symbolized by the seven seas, only *represents* what the Christian mission is; it does not exhaust it. Ocean trips have never made Christian missionaries and, in itself, salt water never will.

Martin Luther made essentially the same point, in the tradition of the fathers of the church, when he asked in *Der grosse Katechismus* in connection with another question: "*Was solt ein handvol wassers der seelen helffen?*" That is, how can a handful of water help the soul? Whether it is a handful or an oceanful, it is still just water. Only when the word is fastened to the element does it become sacramental; as Luther quotes

Augustine: *"Accedat verbum ad elementu et fit sacramentum."* In other words, whether one is considering the sacrament of baptism or the missionary enterprise, form without content is meaningless; the element without the intention is void. Water indeed is not magical, nor is it sacred; but it is sacral.

There are several reasons why the mythological character of the geographical frontier needs to be stressed. In the first place, travel can be a way of going out to meet the world. But it can also be a means of running away from the world. Missionary vocation can become confused with wanderlust:

> What care I for my house and my land?
> What care I for my money, O?
> What care I for my new-wedded lord?
> I'm off with the wraggle-taggle gipsies, O.
>
> English Ballad

It may not always be easy to distinguish gypsies from pilgrims, but the fact that they are both moving, sometimes in the same direction, does not in itself signify they are of the same breed. Even seen through the pious hagiographic filters of missionary biography, many so-called missionary heroes evidently bore indelible marks of the adventurer, the explorer, the wanderer. An 1897 issue of the *Missionary Herald* contained the story of "A Christian Knight-Errant and Hero" who as a child, hearing of the adventures of a missionary in the West Indies in a great storm, said: "I will be a bishop, Mother, and I will have a hurricane, too."

This fact does not necessarily detract from their accomplishments or deprecate their sincerity, because they were in most instances unaware of the mixture of drives that motivated them. David Livingstone, one of the greatest explorers of all time—and primarily a missionary, by the way—was more perceptive than many of his missionary contemporaries when he affirmed to a rally in England: "I go back to Africa, to try and make an open path for commerce and Christianity." Such perceptiveness often accompanies naiveté. This naiveté, however, is only tolerable when it is honest, as it was with Livingstone and most of the great missionary pioneers of the eighteenth and nineteenth centuries. Today, both historical knowledge and psychological insight make naiveté more difficult to preserve, and therefore honesty more difficult to maintain.

In some ways it appears that the foreign missionary enterprise originated as an escape from the evangelistic problems the Western churches faced at home: again, not necessarily a conscious form of escapism, but a subconscious feeling of inability to cope with the new worlds—political, social, economic, and intellectual—which the radical revolutions in these areas were creating in the West and which were threatening the Christian establishments at their very foundations. Official representatives of the churches were not the only ones to be distressed by these challenges. The whole atmosphere of the time was permeated with the spirit of adventure, a spirit that was illustrated in every field of human endeavor. For example, much poetry of the time rang with the longing to wander:

Henceforth I whimper no more, postpone no more,
  need nothing,
Done with indoor complaints, libraries, querulous
  criticisms,
Strong and content I travel the open road.
                    Walt Whitman, *Song of the Open Road*

When evangelical Christians surveyed the mysterious
new worlds opening, their fascination was compounded
of shock at the "barbarism," "deviltry," "ignorance" of
dark heathendom together with a grudging admiration
and even envy of the "innocence," "simplicity," "integrity" of the noble savages. It often appeared to them—
probably most often subconsciously—that here were
worlds in which the problems were simpler, in which
the line dividing good from evil was more sharply
drawn, in which the distinction between Christianity
and paganism was self-evident. They promised a welcome relief from the cross-currents of faith and unbelief that marked the religious scene of their "Christian"
homelands where, if there were missionary frontiers, it
was almost impossible to delineate them or to know
where one might take one's position to defend the faith
or attack the strongholds of Satan.

The missionary movement has had more than its fair
share of those like Father Thomas in Graham Greene's
A Burnt-Out Case, who confesses: "When I finished at
the seminary I sometimes thought that only by martyrdom I could save myself—if I could die before I lost
everything" and whose vocational conclusion drawn
from this complex is: "I wanted to be sent to China. . . ."
Greene's analysis is accurate, for China, perhaps more

than any other of the classic mission fields, has exerted a hypnotic influence on the pietistic missionary imagination, as a kind of Platonic ideal of what a true mission field is. The point is that not only for Father Thomas, the overscrupulous enthusiast, has a vocational martyr complex been projected into the idea of foreign missionary service. The geographical frontier provided for many in the churches a type of symbolic hope of a world in which the relation of the religious and the secular would be as clearly marked off as it was in their bifurcated religious imagination, but which the reality of life in their customary spiritual abodes constantly contradicted. They thought they would meet the "real" world when they went abroad. With that presupposition, of course, they only succeeded in evading it more thoroughly than before. The missionary compound ghetto is the institutional embodiment of that hermetic mentality, just as the sea seemed the only remedy for all its troubles.

But the need to emphasize the mythological character of the geographical frontier arises also from a second, even more important, reason. The Christian imagination had excruciating difficulty in coming to terms with the new cosmological dimensions suggested by Galileo, Copernicus, and their scientific allies. But in a less spectacular, more pervasive way (perhaps because it impinges more directly on empirical, common sense experience and runs more obviously counter to man's introverted parochialism), the complexities of the scientific multidimensional image of the world with its infinite variety of frontiers have been consistently rejected by the Christian religious imagination. One might say that only in the nineteenth century did the Christian common mind put aside the mentality of the patristic age which had condemned the opinion that human beings lived at the antipodes, or that they could have descended from Adam and been saved by Christ, and accepted the new geography's view that the Roman Empire was not the entire *orbis terrarum*. But having accepted this new geographical perspective, the Christian imagination fixed on it in turn.

Popular piety, an accurate index in such matters, still concentrates on the geographical frontier in its devotional exercises, usually to the exclusion of all others. On occasions intended to celebrate missionary concern, this hymn is still likely to be sung.

> From Greenland's icy mountains,
> From India's coral strand,
> Where Afric's sunny fountains
> Roll down their golden sand,
> From many an ancient river,
> From many a palmy plain,
> They call us to deliver
> Their land from error's chain.
>
> Reginald Heber, 1819

Another geographical hymn is often used:

> Nations afar, in ignorance deep;
> Isles of the sea, where darkness lay;
> These hear His voice, they wake from sleep,
> And throng with joy the upward way.
>
> John Julian, 1883

The geographical myth, then, is in part a lens that corrected the inadequate myopic imaginative vision of the church in regard to the field of its mission, but a lens that had its own blind spots and astigmatic distortions ground in. Above all, it provided (to borrow photographic terminology) a flat field of view which lacked plasticity and multidimensional quality.

A fuller appreciation of the meaning of the oneness of the church liberates us from the restrictions of the exclusively geographic idea of the missionary frontier while at the same time maintaining, and even heightening, the sense of missionary constraint. It is the whole world, and not any specified geographical segments of it, that is the mission field of the church. There is only one world and only one church for it. If the missionary frontier is conceived in purely geographical terms, conceivably the mission of the church might eventually be finished. As Bishop J. E. Lesslie Newbigin writes:

Livingstone's picture of the smoke of a thousand villages which had never heard the Gospel, provided that symbol in an age when the world was being opened up by the white man. . . . It does not now correspond to the realities of the world we live in . . . there are no more unknown areas of the world's surface.[4]

The geographical frontier can have meaning and evocative power for missionary obedience if it is understood as a symbol—a symbol of the *total* mission of the one church to the one world. The present task is to draw out the implications of the symbol in such a way that the whole church, wherever it is locally manifested, becomes aware that *it* is in the mission field—the world —and that *it* has the missionary task of carrying the gospel to any and all frontiers. One aspect of the oneness of the church is that every part of the church is at one with the other parts in missionary engagement in the world. In this sense, churches cannot have missions. The church as a whole cannot *have* missions—the implication being that it might *not* have. The church *is* mission. Wherever the church meets the world, *there* is the missionary frontier. And when it crosses frontiers, horizontal or vertical, it does so, not as a "mission," but as the church. Indeed, it is thus that the church proves that it *is* the church.

2

THE CULTURAL MYTH
AND THE
HOLINESS OF THE CHURCH

It's a strange Christianity we have here, but I wonder whether the Apostles would find it as difficult to recognize as the collected works of Thomas Aquinas. If Peter could have understood those, it would have been a greater miracle than Pentecost, don't you think? Even the Nicaean Creed—it has the flavour of higher mathematics to me.

Graham Greene, *A Burnt-Out Case*

ONE OF THE CONCOMITANTS OF THINKING OF THE MISSION frontier as identical with the geographical limits of Western imperial expansion was the idea that this line also divided the world between Christianity and paganism. The missionaries began to think of themselves not only as ambassadors of Christ but also as embodiments of the "Christian way of life."

41

Laurens van der Post, one of the most sensitive interpreters of non-Western cultures, writes of Africa:

We force the African continually to take from us and prevent him from giving to us in his own rich way. We deny Africa its own unique creativeness. It is this frustration which is inflaming primitive man in Africa in the individual as well as the collective sense. . . . The missionary, either in the van or close behind, came to abolish the black man's spirits, give him a new sense of sin, do away with his practice of religion, as base superstitions, and win him over to a new and superior white god. The rejection of Africa in all dimensions was as complete as it could possibly be. . . . I am old enough to remember the enormous hush that fell over Africa in the wake of the coming of European man.[1]

As the missionary movement became increasingly institutionalized, the personal habits and behavior of the missionary as well as the institutions he established were considered to be Christian.

In theory "evangelization" still was the primary aim, but the whole idea of the content of the Christian message was revolutionized: Saving souls involved building communities and institutions that would demonstrate that salvation is not merely for another world but for the transfiguration of society and morals on this earth. With pardonable exaggeration the missionaries preached "Christian civilization."[2]

It is curious that the approach of pietism at the beginning of the Protestant missionary era, as well as that of the proponents of the social gospel in later years, despite their many differences, are quite similar in their attitude to non-Western cultures. This may simply show that religious or theological factors were relatively ineffective in dissipating the arrogance and superiority that have been characteristic of the West in its relations with other cultures in all areas of life. Or it may just be typical of the attitude of conquerors in general all through history.

In the case of pietism, however, cultural insensitivity may have deeper theological roots. The pietist movement, one of the most dynamic and creative in modern church history, with its strong emphasis on the inner life and personal commitment, was the source of vigorous renewal in many churches, not least in the arousing of missionary concern within them. The powerful impact of pietism on the missionary movement, as both an energizing force and a continuing ideological influence, is well known. In a real sense, pietism *made* the Protestant missionary enterprise. At the same time, the spirit of pietism carried with it an ascetic bent, a quietistic attitude toward the cultural order, and a sociological acquiescence that left the "secular" sphere outside of direct Christian responsibility. This sociocultural passivity of the pietist movement, together with a narrowly individualistic understanding of evangelism and ethics, meant that the subtle cultural complexities inherent in missionary activity in foreign lands were ignored. J. H. Bavinck, the Dutch missiologist, says that it showed

. . . in its first attack upon the world a remarkable hostility to the cultural side of the missionary task. It made an effort to limit this task to the proclamation of the message of the grace that is in Jesus Christ. "Winning souls for the Lamb" was the motto which Count von Zinzendorf set for all missionary work. These Pietistic missionaries confined themselves to preaching to individuals whom they sought to impress with the eternal judgment of God. For this very reason they often stood in a negative position over against questions of culture and social relationships. Such matters in their estimation tended only to draw the attention away from the message of grace.[3]

Despite the intention of such a missionary, however, "without being aware of it, he gradually becomes the initiator of a cultural revolution."[4] These oversimplified misconceptions of the missionary task were refuted both by the subsequent developments in the growth of the new "younger" churches, which were obviously both Christian *and* Westernized, and by the evidence accumulated by anthropological research of the intimate connection between religious and cultural life, through which it became clear that it was not possible to provide new religious foundations without toppling the cultural superstructure. To take one example: Among the Bataks in Sumatra the traditional house is—in its graceful form, in its threefold structure, in the symbolic significance of the colors used to decorate it—a representation of the cosmology of the old animism. The story is told of one of the missionaries being asked: "We know concerning everything exactly how we should do it, but when we follow you, we know nothing any more. If we accept your book, how shall we *then* build our houses?" What could be a more poignant critique of the inadequacies of the pietist cultural myth?

In the face of such searching questions, involving the deepest dilemmas of the relation of Christ to culture, the pietistically oriented missionary movement has offered on more than one occasion highly bizarre "solutions" to the problem. As J. C. Furnas writes of the evangelistic efforts in the South Seas:

These missionaries were inescapably as much European petty bourgeois or "mechanics" with an ascetic bent as they were ministers of the Word. They came to the South Seas freighted not only with the doctrine of salvation through the blood of Jesus Christ our Lord, but also with all the arbitrary moral attitudes of Manchester or Hartford, Conn. Nobody ever told them, nor could they have understood, that the Gospel did not necessarily have anything to do with the desirability of plastered walls. The Gospel was one feature of white culture as the missionaries knew it at home; another was a concern with saving one's soul; a third was regular hours of work. Unquestioning, the missionary inculcated all three.[5]

Let us look at another example, this time from Africa:

Missionaries with pietistic backgrounds are prepared to suspect that everything the local people do is bad and that therefore, in order to save them, they must pull them out and set up another kind of life opposed to the original one. This process seldom if ever works, and when it does the result is the creation of a society which consists of converted

45

souls, but no converted life. The missionary under these circumstances takes the path of least resistance, keeps himself untouched by the world and of course does not get into touch with the world in order to save it. . . . The missionary who has been brought up in a closed environment in his home town, has gone away to a church college, and proceeded then to a seminary, is usually still blissfully ignorant of the very life of his own country. He carries this wall of insulation from the world to the mission field and surreptitiously invites anyone who dares to slip inside with him. For this poor soul political questions are dangerous, sex is evil, and academic thought is suspect. . . . So extreme does this loss of touch with the world become that missions have been guilty of making demands on people that tend to separate them from any hope of living the Christian witness among their own people. . . . The children of catechists in one mission in Central Africa are required by the mission rules to wear clothes. The fact that this puts them into a special socio-economic class where they demand more and more money to buy clothes and live up to the class they have been forced into appears to the mission as wanton materialism. In another mission in French Equatorial Africa all catechists were required recently to sign a statement that if they joined a political party they would lose their jobs. These same missionaries most likely never voted in an election and now they are asking their converts to take up the same ignorant attitude toward the State which they have.

It is small wonder, this observer says, that much of Protestant mission work in Africa is considered as "the attempt to form *un état dans l'état*."[6]

Yet another witness to the same phenomenon may be cited:

For example, an Aro of Eastern Nigeria described to my wife how, when a local chief embraced Christianity, he was expected to put all his wives away save one; but it was thought quite unnecessary that he should make any provision for the loneliness or even the subsistence of his former wives. The missionaries stopped all native dancing, whether this was for religion (to which they could rightly object) or for recreation. And the custom of shaming people who had offended against local moral standards by vigorous and ribald lampoons they dismissed as mere bawdry, though in fact it was one of the strongest sanctions to keep behavior up to the mark. Again, in the name of decency, many peoples have been forced into the wearing of ugly and unsuitable clothes, of no more genuine decency than the scantier traditional garments, often to the great worsening of their health. C. P. Mountford (in *Brown Men and Red Sand*) describes how the wearing of European clothes has caused an enormous increase in the death rate from colds and pneumonia, since the clothes will not dry off after the violent showers that occur from time to time.[7]

To explain this cultural insensitivity on the part of many missionaries, the same writer argues that it is inevitable since such cultural awareness is "unlikely to go with the burning faith and zeal that will make a man go out" in missionary service in the first place. This is not the point at which to discuss whether a zealous missionary spirit and cultural consciousness can be successfully married. They probably cannot *if* missionary concern is supposed to be generated only out of pietistic spirituality. But is there not reason for hoping that a more culturally relevant and more theologically founded spirituality may not be capable of producing the same degree of passion and zeal that pietism has evoked in its narrow concentration on saving souls and inner devotional cultivation? Is there not the possibility of a "neopietism" that might embrace both the emphasis on personal faith and obedience and an acute awareness of social, political, and cultural existence?

Some encouragement may be taken from the fact that many of the sharpest criticisms of the cultural myth in missions is being made in missionary journals by missionaries themselves, and not only by hostile journalists or anthropologists as was true so often in the past. Nevertheless, there is still cause for considerable disquiet on this issue. In an article on "Roman Catholic Missionary Methods" which appeared in the *International Review of Missions* in 1914, Bishop Le Roy is quoted as saying:

The missions of the apostolic period and of the Middle Ages made no concessions with regard to doctrine or morals, but in other respects conformed as far as possible to the ways of the people who were being evangelized. At the present day, however, all these peoples, so entirely different from ourselves, are expected to conform to our ways of thinking and doing things, and are compelled to receive Christianity itself, even as regards the smallest details, in an exclusively European form. In view of the results of this method of missionary work, which seem to come very near to failure, one is inclined to ask with some anxiety whether we are really pursuing a right system, and whether it is actually necessary, in order to convert the world, first of all to Latinize it.

Some pride might be taken in such prophetic utterances, especially being granted the sanction of publication in respectable missionary journals—except that they seem to have had such little effect on the subsequent course of events in the missionary movement. The missionary movement still seems committed to the system of Latinizing the world before converting it, or at least while doing so.

D. T. Niles of Ceylon writes of the indelible mark of "Westernity" of contemporary Christianity, and especially of the base of its missionary activity:

Christianity is a Western religion because . . .
—The ecclesiastical forms of the Christian faith as found in the world to-day are largely the result of the history of the churches of the West. . . .
—The decisive role of the churches of the West in determining the shape of things to come.[8] [Italics his]

This is, admittedly, how things look to at least one member of a so-called younger church—though, it must be added, to one who has unparalleled breadth of ecumenical experience on which to base his observations. The fact is that, despite generations of contact with non-Western cultures and intimate involvement in the church life in non-Western lands, Christianity *is* Western. It shows remarkably few marks—liturgically, organizationally, theologically—of being a universal com-

49

munity, with the cultural diversity those words imply.

As D. T. Niles hints, this cultural restriction of the established churches may go far to explain not only the history of sectarian fragmentation in Christianity, but more particularly the rise of such indigenous Christian offshoots as the No-Church movement in Japan, the prophetic sects in Africa, and the eccentric syncretistic groups such as Chris-lam in Indonesia at the present time. In a day of heightened nationalistic self-consciousness, the very suspicion that Western powers are determining the shape of things to come can become inflammatory and cause splintering. But the deeper feeling that somehow the whole cultural ethos of the churches is effectively denying oneself and one's community of their "own unique creativeness," to quote van der Post again, can easily lead either to passive resignation or to rebellion. In the last analysis, the latter reaction may prove to be the most redemptive for the life of the churches in both East and West, North and South, perplexing as it may be to know how best to come to terms with such mercurial and usually divisive movements.

It is no secret how this appears in the eyes of the non-Christians in other parts of the world. Ghandi wrote in 1940: "The moment a person turns a Christian he becomes a *sahib log*. He almost changes his nationality. He gets a job and a position that he could not otherwise have got; he adopts foreign dress and ways of living. He cuts himself off from his own people. . . ." K. M. Pannikar, former Indian ambassador to China, echoes this with his charge that the "missionary onslaught" succeeded only because of "the association of Christian missionary work with aggressive imperialism . . . [and] Western and American cultural aggression." It may be that the fear of cultural aggression is deeper than the fear of religious aggression among most people, ourselves included, and erects a greater barrier to evangelization, a barrier that, ironically, is artificial and need not exist! St. Paul acknowledges the intellectual integrity of the Athenian philosophers and the authentic insights of their poets; he reserves his wrathful cultural critique for the "chosen" who suppose that cultural continuity and ethical traditionalism form a guarantee of orthodoxy and a substitute for a living faith. But even the primitive Christian community, as evidenced in the decisions of the Jerusalem Council, was not prepared to fully accept that radical insight. The later history of the church has been much the same: a vacillating tale of reluctant cultural fundamentalism and cultural timidity, fearful of the world and inhibited in coming to grips with it.

There is a certain perennial quality in the picture of cultural introversion of the Christian community presented by a bishop of the Church of South India, David Chellapa:

Is our worship Indian? . . . the externals of worship, such as architecture and music . . . cannot be ruled out, because it is they which, among other things, help or hinder the impression that Christianity is exotic or native. . . . Church buildings continue to be built in bastard Gothic and in a deliberately and aggressively foreign style. . . . If there has been a difference since 1947, it is probably for the worse, especially where decisions have rested with Indian Christians, as these native Christian gentlemen are often more British and American than the British and Americans themselves! Recently, an Indian revivalist went to conduct a retreat at an ashram, and he sniffed at the beautiful Dravidian Christian temple there, obviously Christian, with a large cross surmounting the *gopuram* and devoid of idols and of all heathen symbolism. But all that revivalist brother could do was to roundly accuse the brethren of trying to please the Hindus and not the Lord Jesus. To the poor, ignorant, misguided man, the style of architecture known as Gothic (which means "pagan") was apparently more Christian, because forsooth it came from the West, from whence was imported his brand of Christianity.[9]

As Bishop Chellapa suggested to his synod, this copying of Western cultural forms might be thought to be a relatively harmless phenomenon. But it has deeper implications, which are potentially destructive of the understanding of the essentials of the faith. Forms that give, or have given, expression to the faith of one people or of one time, may suggest a totally different meaning to another people, in another time. They are, in short, not just culturally inadequate but spiritually misleading:

Our people, too, are naturally reverent, but the unimaginative Protestant missionary has well nigh destroyed their innate *bhakti* by teaching them to pray, not standing, or prostrating, or kneeling, but sitting, even sprawling—not in silence, but always jabbering. . . . Such pernicious and ir-reverent habits have helped to develop pride in a people, naturally humble, and made the Almighty unduly familiar to them, not as the one who is both Transcendent and Im-manent.[10]

What can be said to these things? How can the cul-tural myth of the "Christian way of life" be exorcized?

There is, for one thing, the need to cultivate a spirit of cultural humility. Cultural arrogance is all too eas-ily bolstered and rationalized by religious and theologi-cal superiority complexes. St. Paul asserts that we are not to "preach ourselves," and this surely includes our cultural selves, individual and communal. A blue-eyed, blond, Nordic Jesus depicted in a painting at the front of a theological seminary chapel in Madagascar is not just a quaint cultural anachronism reflecting the insularity and naiveté of the pioneer missionaries; he is, in fact, a vivid symbol of a fateful Christological heresy that denies one of the foundation stones of the Christian tradition, the Incarnation.

On purely humanistic grounds it is appropriate to as-sert that "not only a spoon and fork spell civilization" and find "that Chinese food tastes better with chop-sticks and Indonesian food tastes better eaten with the fingers." As an old Malay once told Sir Hugh Clifford: "I'm quite sure my fingers have not been in anybody else's mouth, but I'm not so sure about your spoons." This kind of cultural tolerance can spring from the open, educated, experienced mind. But even without that, the Christian adopts the same attitude because he has been taught that in Christ there is no "bar-barian."

For another thing, there is a need to recognize that there is no one way of life for the Christian. Sharp criticism has been directed against styles of life which have been considered the ultimate expression of Christian discipline and obedience but which have become outmoded by social changes, cultural shifts, and theological emphases. The conclusion sometimes drawn—that what is needed is a contemporary Christian "style of life" more appropriate to these changes and outlooks—naturally occurs to the culturally tolerant mind, but it is not a particularly Christian insight. Indeed, the search for a new, modern, relevant, Christian style of life which has obsessed many may actually be a kind of sublimated pietism, with its characteristic presupposition that the essence of the gospel is an ethical rule and that salvation is measured by the extent to which it may be approximated in daily life. It is in fact a recrudescence of Pelagian works-righteousness in sophisticated, modern form. The early Dietrich Bonhoeffer, later liberated in many ways, from whom neo-pietists take their lead, is on this point, with his stress on discipleship, all too clearly a child of classical pietism. He insistently posits a universal moral standard—however obscure and difficult to decipher—by which all Christian ways of life are to be estimated and judged. Unfortunately, Bonhoeffer's own self-correction at this point does not seem to have affected his most ardent neo-pietist followers: "For a long time I did not realise how far we were apart. I thought I could acquire faith by trying to live a holy life, or something like it. It was in this phase that I wrote *The Cost of Discipleship*. Today I can see the dangers of this book, though I am prepared to stand by what I wrote."[11]

Bonhoeffer's corrective to his inherited, inbred pietist leaning was a growing conviction of the positive value of "a this-worldly life" (which he saw in Luther) and his acceptance of "the adulthood of the world." He increasingly came to see that the Christian

. . . must live a "Worldly" life and so participate in the suffering of God. He *may* live a worldly life as one emancipated from all false religions and obligations. To be a Christian does not mean to be religious in a particular way, to cultivate some particular form of asceticism (as a sinner, a penitent, or a saint), but to be a man. . . . There is nothing of religious asceticism here. The religious act is always something partial, faith is always something whole, an act involving the whole life.[12]

Thus, holiness is understood as something that transcends and overflows ethical or religious categories. To be holy is to be a man, a man of the world, and above all to be alive. Says Bonhoeffer: "Jesus does not call men to a new religion, but to life. . . . The Christian is not a *homo religiosus*, but a man, pure and simple, just as Jesus was a man, compared with John the Baptist anyhow."[13]

This revolutionary interpretation of holiness, which represents such a radical break with the pietist tradition (and with its counterpart, according to Bonhoeffer, in existentialist philosophy and psychotherapy, which he termed "secularized methodism"), has enormous emancipation potentialities for the traditional spirit and forms of the foreign missionary enterprise. To mention but one of them: the obsessive fear of syncretism, which has always plagued the missionary movement and is even evident in such a wise and perceptive missionary statesman as Hendrik Kraemer in his approach to "nonchristian" religions and cultures, must be radically reappraised. The classical conception of missionary vocation equally requires a profound rescrutiny in this light, a subject to be dealt with in a later chapter.

This new recognition of the autonomy of man is closely related to a more trinitarian theological orientation over against the "Jesus-cult" religion (to use Donald Baillie's term) of pietism and evangelicalism, and eventually dictates a new Christian posture in regard to both culture and morals.

It is obviously impossible to base this kind of understanding of holiness on a narrow Christo-monism. True, it rests on fundamental Christological principles: on the anthropological affirmation of the classical creeds that Jesus Christ is "true man" and on the biblical insistence that "the Word became flesh and dwelt among us." But it leaves us in the ambivalent position of not really knowing enough about *how* he dwelt among us to be provided with an adequate archetypal pattern of a Christian style of life to direct our moral and cultural ways with absolute precision and clarity. For example, the "silent years" of Jesus' life—the eighteen years between his appearance in the temple and the beginning of his active ministry—are crucial if we are to seek to follow in his footsteps as a secular and worldly man.

We may say, with John Oman, that Jesus' ministry was itself preeminently secular and that its distinctiveness lay in meeting, in the ordinary course of life and along the normal pathways of man, secular problems in a theological manner. But the strange biblical silence about a large period of Jesus' secular history leaves us with many unanswered questions if we seek to find practical guidance in these matters through his example. It underlines the need for defining holiness in Trinitarian terms.

On one hand, holiness must be understood in light of the fact that God created the world. Neither the doctrine of the fall nor modern reappropriations through psychology and literature of the reality of the demonic can obscure the primal fact that "the earth is the Lord's and the fullness thereof." The stance of the Christian in the world is that of one who knows that the world and they who dwell in it are God's handiwork. It is therefore an affirmative stance. However deep his recognition of the alienations and ambiguities resulting from sin, his attitude is ultimately hopeful, for he knows that "all things work together for him who loves God," and he carries a vision not of the destruction and ultimate denial of the world but of a new creation—and that not only of a new heaven but also a renewed earth.

It is this theological ground, not a sentimental-romantic one, that determines the manner and spirit of "identification." Identification is a necessary prerequisite for missionary engagement, but the missionary movement has constantly been perplexed, not knowing how to go about it or how far it should be carried. In essence, identification depends on acceptance of the integrity of other cultures, other modes of thought, other ways of life, because they are seen as expressions of God's creative intentions for the world.

Joseph Kitagawa describes what this means in practice:

We must remind ourselves that Western categories and Western modes of thinking are not the best or most reliable tools for our attempt to understand the religions and cultures of Asia. This does not mean that there are no universal elements in human experience and cognition. All men everywhere go through the same cycles of life, such as birth, naming, initiation, marriage, sickness and recovery, war and peace, death and burial. But the ways of structuring these experiences are not the same universally. As Lily Abegg points out (Ostasiens denkt anders), Asians have their own perspectives from which they interpret the events of life and the meaning of history. Those who believe in the transmigration of souls feel the sorrow of parting just as much as anyone else, but they certainly will never say, "O death, where is thy sting?" In fact, "to be raised incorruptible from the dead" is not good news to those who are trying to be delivered from the chain of birth and rebirth. Thus, in order to "understand" Asian peoples, their religions and cultures, one must enter as much as possible into the very structure of their thought and spiritual experience, and this takes more than a sheer intellectual endeavor. Unlike Westerners, who try to grasp the nature of an object "objectively," Easterners are preoccupied more with the act of knowing, or the state of consciousness and cognition, than with the object as such, because to them "knowing" is another form of "being." That is why our effort to "understand" Asians involves a total understanding, implying a sort of *metanoia*.[14]

Thus a new sort of conversion goes along with a new sort of holiness, for both are posited on faith in God the Creator.

On the other hand, holiness must also be understood in light of the fact that the Holy Spirit is life-giver. An understanding of holiness based solely on an understanding of the doctrine of creation could become stagnant and stereotyped. A pneumatological approach provides the needed dynamic element in a new view of holiness.

It has been pointed out that attempts to find archetypal cultural forms in past eras of Christian history, or usable Christian models from other regions, which could be copied or adapted to new situations, are futile. When these attempts are not destructive, they are nearly always ludicrous. But the alternative that Bishop Chellapa and others propose—the adoption and adaptation of indigenous cultural forms—is equally irrelevant. It is of no help to substitute for outmoded Christian cultural forms and patterns of life equally antiquated Hindu ones. What usually happens, however firmly a cross is stuck on the top, is analogous to the incongruity of the Buddhist temple in Rangoon with one of its portals constructed in "bastard Gothic," to use Bishop Chellapa's apt phrase.

In many cases, as with the mock Buddhist monastery Toa-Fun-Shan in Hong Kong erected by the imaginative pioneer missionary, Karl Reichelt of Norway, these strained efforts at "indigeneity" have been initiated by the foreign missionaries themselves. When they are successful architecturally, and are not merely ridiculous monstrosities, they turn out to be anachronistic, with little functional value. They seem to be an expression of the foreignness that the missionary sees in the exotic land where he works. They may even be caricatures. The same type of thing may be seen elsewhere: The liturgical experiments with modern jazz in Western churches have generally fallen flat, not for the reasons usually raised against such experiments on grounds of propriety and tradition, but because the jazz used has generally been either bad or outdated!

The English have a word for this kind of artificial and forced contemporaneity or indigeneity. "Precious," they call it. In American parlance the word is "cute." Romantic, superficial cultural syntheses lack authenticity and integrity. As Frank Lloyd Wright wrote in his plea for organic architecture against the tendency to make style a motive in itself in building:

Half-baked, imitative designs (fictitious semblances) pretentiously put forward in the name of a movement or a cause . . . endanger the cause, weaken the efficiency of genuine work, for the time being at least; lower the standard of artistic integrity permanently; demoralize all values artistically; until utter prostitution results.[15]

Wright wisely perceived that this kind of cultural imitation was at its heart an ethical problem, for as he says, artistic integrity is not just a question of personal relations but has also to do with "relation to sources of inspiration, the finer material the architect uses in shaping the thing he gives to his client."

This insight can be appropriately applied to the cultural myth propagated by the missionary movement, which presupposes a Christian way of life already given and articulated. The fact is that "shaping the thing" is not only decided by tradition or by conformity to existing patterns but is derived from the sources of inspiration directly and existentially. Or to put it theologically: Faith in the continuing life-giving work of the Holy Spirit emancipates us from the deadening burden of the ever-increasing weight of historical tradition as well as from the restrictive pressures of conformity to existing ways and styles, whether of behavior, architecture, or modes of thought.

It is not in architecture, however, that the issue is fully joined. It is in the formulation of theology itself. The churches that have resulted from the missionary activities of the Western churches have been markedly undistinguished in theological creativity. Analogies are often glibly drawn between the development of the "young" churches in primitive Christianity and the "younger" churches arising out of the missionary en-

61

terprise in Asia, Africa, and Latin America. Whatever similarities there may be between these two eras in Christian history in other respects, there is no comparison between them in their theological productivity and originality. As Bishop Chellapa complains: "The Indian Church has not yet produced a single original heresy," and he notes that instead of struggling to find "a theology that is at once Indian and Christian," theological students "bury" themselves in the writings of Western theologians. In spite of all exceptions, theological passivity seems to be the rule among mission churches.

This indicates that the cultural myth has not only obsessed the foreign missionaries, but that their inhibitions have been transferred to the new Christian communities they have fostered. One factor in this is, of course, a purely institutional one. Theological creativity and originality threaten the institutional relations between churches whose connections are denominationally determined, at least insofar as such denominationalism defines itself in terms of traditional Western theological formularies. An illustration of this narrow theological mentality may be found in the dogmatic paroxysms that the Confession of Faith of the Huria Kristen Batak Protestant in Indonesia provoked among many of the vaunted defenders of Lutheran "orthodoxy" in the Western churches. The conception of theological rightness that such confessionalists tend to exhibit is apparently decided exclusively by the extent to which any theological or confessional statements conform to their (Western European) interpretation of the confessional writings of German Christians of the sixteenth and seventeenth centuries.

This kind of narrow mental outlook is also seen in the arguments put forward by the bishops of the Anglican Communion assembled at Lambeth in 1957, in their parochial judgments on the merits of the Church of South India's ministry, and in their attitudes towards other church union schemes in which Anglicans have been involved. It does not seem to occur to such theologians or to their ecclesiastical assemblies how Western they are or how Western the forms they consider orthodox are when seen from another cultural or historical perspective. Above all, it seems beyond their powers of religious imagination to be open to the variety, originality, and spontaneity of theological expressions that are the mark of the continuing work of the Holy Spirit in the life of the ever-changing but ever-catholic church.

This theological provincialism has apparently exerted a depressing effect on the theological creativity of the churches who look to them as their "fathers" in the faith and, perhaps more importantly, still look to them for financial and material support. Theological originality may exact a price from the younger churches which they literally cannot afford to pay at the present time.

This is an impoverishment not only for them, however; the theological catholicity of the whole church is suffering. Austin Farrer writes in *The Glass of Vision:*

The Medieval Scholastic mind, it would seem, was (in theory, at any rate) on the hunt for theological propositions, out of which a correct system of doctrine could be deduced by logical method. . . . It is false in its assumptions, because it supposes that St. Paul or St. John is, after all, a systematic theologian. A very unsystematic theologian no doubt, too impulsive and enthusiastic to put his material in proper order or to standardize his terminology. Still, what of that? Anyone who has a decent modern education can do it for him.[16]

The new theological, as well as ecclesiological, formulations of the younger churches are, as Farrer's ironic words hint, essential not only for their own health and integrity as members of the whole Body of Christ, but for the health and integrity of the whole Body as an entity.

In these and other ways the narrowing vision which accompanied the cultural myth has its amusing aspects. But more seriously, it has too often meant that Christians in the lands of nationalistic and cultural resurgence are not infrequently carrying a double cross: the inevitable and true Christian one but also the "foreign" cross of national and cultural alienation. They have a "continuing city," but it does not happen to be located in Rome, Lambeth, Geneva, Wittenberg, or New York.

3

THE ECCLESIOLOGICAL MYTH AND THE CATHOLICITY OF THE CHURCH

We never do wrong so thoroughly and gaily as when we do so in obedience to conscience.

Pascal

THE VERY TERM "YOUNGER CHURCHES," SO POPULAR IN mission circles, indicates how profoundly the paternal image has stamped itself on the mentality of the missionary movement. It is, of course, a descriptive phrase. But what does it actually describe? A reality? A relationship? A redundancy? One might even say that the term "younger," in preference to the more neutral "young," accentuates this ambiguity, for it implies an evaluative judgment the criterion for which is uncertain and a comparative conclusion the grounds for which are unstated.

At face value, the term could be taken to be chronological. But in missionary usage it is more heavily freighted with meaning. Overtones and undertones of signification give it a mythological character. A subtle transference takes place in which, for example, the term is gradually taken out of its historical context, in which it is chronologically understood, and becomes ideological, ecclesiologically understood.

Whether this is appropriate or inappropriate is the basic problem. As historical institutions, particular churches can mark the dates of their founding. From this chronological perspective the distinction between younger and older has validity. But is it valid to apply the distinction to churches as they are *now*, either in a comparative way between churches or as they are essentially in themselves? In other words, whatever length of time they may have been in existence institutionally, is it appropriate to use such qualifying terms as younger and older in connection with the word "church"? Whether intended or not, this type of distinction made between churches might suggest degrees of "churchity," and if the terms younger and older are so applied they would further imply that the historical passage of time itself was the primary former of churches—a church would be more fully a church because it was older.

This is a highly suspect ecclesiological principle. It might also be said that there is, or was, no such intention in the mind of those who coined the terms, or of those who now use them. But can we be sure? One of the volumes of the Jerusalem Conference (1928) of the International Missionary Council is entitled *Younger and Older Churches*. This was an advance over the practice of distinguishing between missions and churches. Both at Jerusalem and at the subsequent Madras "Tambaram" Conference in 1938, however, it appears that the change in terminology is not matched by any profound ecclesiological reevaluation. In fact, the two sets of terms both seem to reflect the same ecclesiological presupposition: an evolutionary development of churches within a hierarchical ecclesiological pattern. The phrase "partnership in obedience," which arose out of the 1947 Whitby Conference, does suggest a significant ideological shift within the missionary movement, insofar as such meetings can be taken as accurate reflections of the ethos of missions. Nevertheless, the perpetuation of the younger and older dichotomy in considering partnership vitiates much of this advance in mission thinking. It reminds one of Albert Schweitzer's statement: "A word about the relations between the whites and the blacks . . . I have coined the formula: 'I am your brother, it is true, but your older brother.'"

This type of vitiation of ecclesiology by a spirit of cultural superiority and paternalism within the missionary movement has more than theoretical ramifications. A mission apologist writes from a South Seas station: "People often ask why, after 140 years, the Church of Tahiti is not autonomous. . . . It is essential that the president should be of adequate spiritual and intel-

67

lectual calibre, and it is in the interests of the Church as well . . . it is here that the missionaries still have much to do."[1] This casual, almost automatic, equation of spiritual and intellectual caliber evidenced here shows how easily paternalism, with its assumptions of superiority, actually determines missionary policy—particularly if there is no effective inner corrective and counterbalance provided by clear ecclesiological convictions.

This conclusion is substantiated by the length of time that the missionary movement has been aware of the problem, in theory at least. As early as 1913, Dr. A. J. Brown wrote: "It has long been an axiom that the object of the foreign missionary enterprise is to develop a self-governing, self-propagating and self-supporting Church," and he gives the example of the Synod of the Church of Christ in Japan, which in its meetings of 1906 and 1907 established the principle of "co-operation" for foreign missions in Japan: "A co-operating mission is one which recognizes the right of the Church of Christ in Japan to the general control of all evangelistic work done by the mission as a mission within the Church or in connection with it." Such a policy reflects some of the advanced thinking of men like Henry Venn and others in the nineteenth century who recognized the importance of granting independence to newly established churches so that they could mature and become missionary bodies themselves.

But much mission theory remained in the realm of what Alfred North Whitehead called "inert ideas." Dr.

J. Warneck, one of the pioneers of the Batak Mission in Sumatra, wrote in the *International Review of Missions* in 1912 that "Nommensen saw clearly from the first that the native Christian was the best missionary . . . the time must come when [Sumatra] will be able to dispense with any kind of European Christianity, when the missionaries will leave the country because their work is finished." In his I.M.C. Survey of the Batak Church in 1938, however, J. Merle Davis reported:

The mission and the missionary hold a place of authority in the Batak Church. The high degree of centralization in the organization of the Mission has resulted in its playing a paternalistic, if not a dominating part, in the life of the Christian community. . . . Though the Batak Church is called "independent" it is so only in the sense that it is receiving no financial aid from the Mission. This in itself is a remarkable achievement. Although the Great Synod votes on all matters in the control of the Church's funds and in determining its policies and programme, the last word is with the Mission, through the veto power of the General Superintendent, who is Chairman of the Great Synod of the Batak Church.

A large degree of authority is also held by the missionaries who preside over the five districts of the Church. While the power of the Mission is exercised with caution and consideration and while the wisdom and Christian spirit of the missionaries are of a high order, the position is one of danger for the solidarity of the Church and the growth of Batak leadership.

In the World Dominion Survey Series volume *The Netherlands Indies* (1935), much the same situation is reported by Hendrik Kraemer: "The Batak Protestant Church has been organized as an independent Church, but owing to the part still played by the missionaries, does not have full power over its own affairs." It was Davis's opinion that the sectarianism that developed in the Batak Church could be attributed partially to missionary paternalism, which weakened the inner life of the Church: "the paternal system of mission control of Church policies has developed a restiveness within the Church which has resulted in the separating of considerable groups of churches from the Great Synod." Kraemer gives the same explanation for the rise of the separatist movements, the largest of which is the so-called H.K.I.—Huria Kristen Indonesia: "The rebels, owing to the feeling that their ambitions are not approved, do not in consequence have the advice and sympathetic support which would otherwise have been so valuable."

It must be remembered that this is being said of one of the largest autonomous and independent younger churches in the world, one which from the beginning was built up with a minimum of foreign missionary personnel and outside financial assistance and subsidies. In many other cases, missionary paternal control was far more complete and stringent. But even in the case of the Batak Church, the financial policy, which proved wise in the long run, was partly the result of chance rather than deliberate policy, as Kraemer points out:

The founding of the Batak churches coincided with a decade of straitened financial circumstances of the Barmen

Mission. The political and financial tensions in Germany . . . between 1864 and 1871, seriously reduced the strength of the missionary societies. . . . These circumstances, rather than the voluntary withholding of funds, determined the financial policy of the mission. . . . In this way it came about that from the beginning the Bataks took care of their own pastors, built their own churches, and received no financial aid from the mission.

Again, it was through outward circumstances rather than deliberate mission strategy that the Batak Church became not only legally autonomous and independent but psychologically liberated as well. The missionary era ended with the Japanese invasion and occupation during World War II, all foreign missionaries were sent away or interned, and the Indonesian independence struggle against the Dutch culminated in the establishment of the Republic of Indonesia after the war. The law of the republic prohibits control by foreigners of Indonesian institutions.

It should not be assumed that the often cataclysmic end of missionary control of the younger churches through war and revolution, which was the story of Indonesia and many other places since then, necessarily marks the end of missionary paternalistic influence. William A. Smalley writes in *Practical Anthropology*:

There have been shifts and adjustments, but the differences are not necessarily very fundamental . . . the missionaries (whether they are called by that name or not) who previously had political power within the church still have that power. It is exercised in less direct fashion, but it is there. Paternalism in missions is in danger of changing to puppeteering. The fathers have become brothers, but they are brothers who pull strings.[2]

Every meeting of a new ecumenical missionary expression such as the East Asia Christian Conference, however formally it may represent a new equality in relationship and "partnership in obedience," exhibits the subtle and pervasive power of the paternal brothers who pull strings. This may be done in various ways, but the chief continuing source of paternal power is financial. Whether through the advice of a fraternal representative of the World Council of Churches, or through the expressions of budgetary interest in certain aspects of the program by mission board observers, the paternalistic mentality may still be alive and effectively at work. The institutional form may be egalitarian, the epitome of partnership, but the political dynamics may still be paternalistic. The new forms of ecumenical mission are no guarantee that there will not be those operating within them, and even controlling their policies, who "are half-drugged by that sense of their own indispensability and of African inadequacy."[3]

The continuation of the paternalistic mentality in the missionary enterprise justifies the use of the word "myth" to explain it. As has been pointed out, the new ecclesiocentric theory of missions has been in existence for many years. Echoing the ideas of Henry Venn from a half century before, the *International Review of Missions* editorialized in its first issue in 1912:

It was generally recognized at the Edinburgh Conference that the chief factor in missionary work at the present time is the Church in the mission field. In many countries the problem of making Christianity indigenous, and of building up a strong, independent, self-supporting, self-propagating Church is even more pressing than that of securing more foreign missionaries.

But another fifty years passes and Bishop Stephen Neill records the sharp reactions provoked among missionary leaders at the I.M.C. Ghana Conference in 1958 by his call, "Down with missions!"

This peculiar (or normal?) schizophrenic tendency in missionary theory and practice during the twentieth century must be explained in mythological rather than purely rational terms. In this, as in many other recent instances in the Christian community, it is only very gradually that the pietistic confidence in the power of "individual acts of will, dependent on the free decisions of the conscious personality" is "broken down . . . by the new recognition of the destructive mechanisms determining the unconscious trends of individuals and groups."[4] And the almost demonic tenacity of the paternalistic mentality is understandable only when the self-consciously philanthropic motivation lying behind it is appreciated. The paternalist's intention may be all good in his own mind, but (to use William String-fellow's favorite term to explain the impotency of the churches' response to the racial problem in the United States) his "lily-white," optimistic anthropological presuppositions blind him to the possibility that, as Reinhold Niebuhr puts it, "not much evil is done by evil people. Most of the evil is done by good people, who do not know that they are not good. . . . It is one of the true functions of the minister of Christ to puncture the self-deceptions, including his own, by which people try to perpetuate the open secret that we all think of ourselves more highly than we ought to think."[5]

How can this puncturing of self-deceptions be done? And in particular how can it be achieved in relation to paternalism in missions?

In the first place, it may be accomplished by the frank recognition that Christians—including missionaries—*are* like other men. In an individual sense, to say that missionaries are or have been paternalistic is simply to state a psychological truism, as obvious as the fact that human beings always tend to be either domineering or dependent. Pascal writes:

> It is wrong to cling to me, though you do so with pleasure and of free will . . . the object to which you cling will die. . . . And if I invite others to cling to me, whatever benefit I might get, I must warn men on the point of consenting to a lie, that they must not believe it; and similarly that they should not cling to me, for they must spend their lives and their endeavor in pleasing God, or in seeking him.[6]

In a collective sense, to say that the missionary movement has been or is paternalistic is simply to state an historical truism, as obvious as the fact that the whole of the relationship between the Western and non-Western worlds in the eighteenth, nineteenth, and twentieth centuries has been paternalistic. Dependency and in-dependency has been the contrapuntal motif running through their connections ever since they first confronted one another. It is not suprising, therefore, that in a colonial era, for example, or in a colonial context the Christian missionary movement was itself colonial.

That this situation was not entirely bad is shown by Kenneth Ingham's *Reformers in India 1793-1833,* which pays generous tribute to the deep influence of Christian missionaries on Indian social betterment. In almost every area of the world, the philanthropic contributions of the missionaries to the raising of social standards, of economic improvements, of health conditions has been notable. Nevertheless, the recipients, grateful as they were, demanded more. As Bishop Azariah told the delegates at the Edinburgh Conference in 1910: "You have given your goods to feed the poor. You have given your bodies to be burned. We also ask for *love.* Give us *friends."*

In other words, what was finally required was a new relationship. It requires a generous spirit to give; but giving has its own gratifications. An even more generous spirit may be required to receive. Only if the relationship between the giver and the receiver is sound can the giving-receiving connection be healthy: otherwise, both may be corrupted—the giver by pride and the receiver by resentment. It was this fact (to which paternalism is fatally oblivious) that the missionary movement never seemed to fully recognize or appreciate, probably because the whole enterprise was "in obedience to conscience."

The missionary movement's paternalistic blindness on this point was accentuated by the cultural insularity and provincialism characteristic of the West in its whole relationship with the non-Western world, as has already been mentioned. Lord Robins, writing in the London *Times* (March 3, 1959), argued:

First of all, the predominance of the white man—the British white African—must continue for at least another generation. Few black Africans of the central African tribes have yet developed the qualities of leadership, or the education and experience to act without control. . . . Social relations must be governed by good manners, civilized behaviour, and the will of both parties.

Leonard Woolf, commenting on this viewpoint, said:

. . . ninety-nine out of every one hundred white men in Ceylon were saying of the Sinhalese and Tamils precisely what Lord Robins and the white settlers of Salisbury are saying today about the black Africans. They had not, we said, "developed the qualities of leadership, or the education and experience to act without control." If we were looking at politics with the eye of God, we should have to say that we were quite right—they would swindle and cheat and exploit and massacre one another and prove quite conclusively that they are not fit to govern themselves.

Where we were wrong was in thinking that it followed that we ought to govern them. Two world wars and the cold war and Fascism, Nazism, and Communism, and our calendar of crime and racial riots make one doubtful whether Europeans are fit to govern themselves. In the eye of God, which is another way of saying, if you are really concerned with the plain brutal truth, politically and culturally the Europeans and Asiatics have reached two rather different forms of barbarism. The record of our political and social history, even when we govern ourselves, is pretty grim, but we are at least accustomed to govern social relations by our own peculiar form of bad manners and barbarous behaviour. The trouble really begins when one kind of barbarian like Sir Roy Welensky and Lord Robins, no doubt from the highest motives and with the old, old clichés which you can read in Herodotus were being used by the imperialist Xerxes on the Hellespont 2,400 years ago, insists upon imposing by force its own peculiar domestic form of barbarism on a different kind of barbarism—for its own good, and because it is not yet capable of governing itself. . . . Imperialism has always been bad for the imperialists. It always in the end reduces them to the state of mind . . . in which they are no longer capable of facing facts because they believe in their own clichés and mumbo-jumbo.[7]

The idea, often reflected in missionary literature in the past, that the missionaries would know—would be capable of looking with "the eye of God"—when a mission was mature enough, or developed enough to be called a church, is a product of the spirit that Woolf describes. The same might be said of those who believe that the distinction between younger and older churches is self-evident, or that the older should decide which is what.

Of course, force in the sense that Woolf uses it is alien to the missionary enterprise; but power is not. Paternalism in missions has been backed up by power, financial if nothing else. Again, this has generally been exercised with restraint, but not always with sensitivity.

The political and institutional weakness of missionary strategy in regard to "devolution" can be traced to a theological flaw. St. Paul wrote to the Christians at Corinth: "We preach not ourselves. . . ." The difficulty is to know what constitutes ourselves. How can we clearly distinguish between that witness, or institutional form, or organizational pattern, which reflects what we are and that which reflects who Christ is? How can we be critical of our own barbarisms?

Paul Tillich writes:

The idea of the demonic is the mythical expression of a reality that was in the centre of Luther's experience as it was in Paul's namely, the structural, and therefore inescapable power of evil . . . beyond the moral power of good will, producing social and individual tragedy precisely through the inseparable mixture of good and evil in every human act.[8]

With its inadequate theological footings, the missionary movement tended to be unaware of this inseparable mixture, not only in its preaching but even more in its organizational life. The average missionaries did not see that insofar as the missionary response is a human act, it incorporates this contemporary analysis of human nature, both Christian and secular analyses. But in the missionary enterprise with its pietistic leanings, the missionary response was interpreted almost exclusively in personal terms: sin, justification, sanctification, in the inner life of the believer. What was not seen with equal clarity was that Tillich's words also apply to the organizational and institutional aspects of Christian existence. The mixed character of Christian institutions and movements is not demonic in itself, for the demonic element lies not so much in the inseparable and inescapable character of the mixture, as Tillich defines it, as in the failure to admit that the mixture exists and that it is inescapable.

One corrective to this sociological and psychological naiveté of missions in its approach to the problem of the relationship between mission and church, or between younger and older churches, is found in the willingness to face the plain brutal truth. But radical self-criticism has a largely negative function. It must be supplemented by a positive principle for action and policy in the present and future. Old paternalistic demons cast out, however clean the room is swept, will be replaced by others—less barbaric but no less demonic.

In the second place, therefore, the old ecclesiological myth must be replaced by a true ecclesiology. The past and present self-deceptions of the missionary movement must be examined before future tasks can be approached. It is important to see how the missionary movement has succeeded, and to learn from those successes. More important, at the moment, may be to see how the missionary movement has failed, and to learn from those failures. The faulty ecclesiology of the missionary movement, with its superficial understanding of the corporate and catholic character of the church, weakened its awareness of the fact that the lofty character of the missionary calling is no guarantee against demonic penetration, but a peculiarly favorable spiritual climate for its effective invasion and domination, and that "holy" institutions have a special tendency, in proclaiming Christ, to preach themselves.

In the ecclesiological perspective, the paternal image is not entirely inappropriate. One may cite the apostolic sanction of Saint Paul himself, who writes to the Corinthian Christians "to admonish you as my beloved children. For though you have countless guides in Christ, you do not have many fathers. For I became your father in Christ Jesus through the gospel." At the same time, as has been said, the paternal metaphor in missionary circles may be considered a symptom of a political and cultural superiority complex, and even spiritual arrogance.

On the biblical-theological level, therefore, there must be a reexamination of the validity of the paternal relation as a pattern for interchurch affairs. Can Saint Paul's personal position as "father" to the converts at Corinth be applied to the relation between, for example, the church at Jerusalem and the church at Corinth or Antioch? Is there a paternal succession from one missionary generation to another? Paul's references to guides would seem to indicate otherwise. And Christ's injunction, "Call no man your father on earth, for you have one Father, who is in heaven," must be taken into consideration.

On the socio-institutional level, there must be a radical reassessment of the adequacy of the traditional distinction between younger and older churches and the even earlier one between missions and churches. Even in the eyes of an enlightened paternalism, can it be held that a church evolves or devolves out of a mission? When is a church fully a church? Is there any *ecclesiological* justification for the distinction between younger and older?

From these perspectives, and on sound ecclesiological grounds, the paternal image applied to the institutional relations of the missionary enterprise seems highly questionable. Mission history illustrates how this faulty ecclesiological position becomes an implicit theological rationale for the perpetuation of foreign control over missions and younger churches, and an unconscious justification for the permanency of the foreign missionary enterprise in its traditional institutional and structural forms, however anachronistic and self-defeating they may be.

An ecclesiological renewal of the missionary movement *might* rehabilitate some of the old forms and structures of the missionary enterprise. But if this ecclesiological reappraisal shows the inappropriateness of certain forms in their very origin, or their anachronistic character through the passage of time, these institutional patterns must be put aside and new forms must be sought to incarnate the new ecclesiological principle that the church is catholic. In this Body there is only one Head—for all the members.

4

THE VOCATIONAL MYTH AND THE APOSTOLICITY OF THE CHURCH

The virtue of a symbol lies, and always did lie, in a relative degree of unintelligibility. A symbol loses its grip once its significance has been rationalized, and it has become generally understood. But so long as it remains unintelligible, it can, if it is a good symbol, exercise astonishing powers. These powers are by no means necessarily confined to a restricted circle of initiates—the effectiveness of symbols is in fact proportionate to their collectivity—to the range of significance they have for the collective unconscious.

Herbert Read, *The Grass Roots of Art*

IT WOULD BE DIFFICULT TO OVERESTIMATE THE ASTONISH-ing power the foreign missionary has exercised as a symbol for the collective unconscious of Western Christianity. Indeed, the same might be said of the symbolic significance of the white missionary for Western secu-

82

lar man as well. The symbolic meaning of the missionary is obviously not exactly the same for the church as it is for the secular world. But it is not entirely different either. In fact, it may be in the attitude of secular man to the missionary and his endeavors that the real unconscious attitude of the church is disclosed as well.

Albert Schweitzer's popular appeal as a missionary symbol has always been a source of some astonishment to the missionary and ecclesiastical establishment, particularly since Schweitzer's individualistic approach as well as his radical theological orientation has been something of an embarrassment to it. Nevertheless, it is indisputable that no other individual in this generation has so captured the Western imagination—especially that of the Western intellectuals—as the embodiment of missionary vocation. The point is that the fascination this man has exerted on the popular mind is due not so much to his actual accomplishments or to the special character of his work but to the simple fact that he has become a symbol. Furthermore, some of the very things that alienate him from the ecclesiastical and missionary establishment—his cultural and intellectual sophistication, his self-dramatization with its public relations overtones, his adoption of the external trappings of classical foreign missionary style, his mystical and vitalistic philosophy so congenial to secular humanism—are the things that commend him as a symbol to the secular intelligentsia, itself alienated from the established religious institutions of the West but still subconsciously clinging to many of the ideals that those institutions have traditionally propogated. Above all, his dramatic renunciation of distinguished careers in music, philosophy, and theology had a quality of absurdity, or unintelligibility, giving it an unparalleled symbolic grip on the Western post-Christian mind, which had increasingly become aware (partly through Schweitzer's own philosophical writings) of the dead and perhaps demonic ends into which secularism without any religious elevation was leading Western civilization.

In previous generations, when the cleavage between the Christian and the secular communities was not so pronounced in the West, the "standard" foreign missionary served much the same kind of symbolic function for the whole of Western society. Not long after William Carey had begun his heroic pioneering work in India, Sidney Smith in the *Edinburgh Review* of April 1807 scornfully satirized those "consecrated cobblers" who foolishly thought to convert India. But Robert Southey, in spite of being a high churchman, responded in the first number of the *Quarterly Review:* "In fourteen years these low-born, low-bred mechanics have done more to spread the knowledge of the Scripture among the heathen than has been accomplished, or even attempted, by all the princes and potentates of the world, and all the universities and establishments into the bargain."

One sees in this exchange between Smith and Southey the ambivalent feelings that have existed both within and outside the churches about the missionary enterprise. There is a certain condescension toward the missionary as a person, yet, combined with it, there is a grudging admiration for his heroic spirit. There is, as well, both annoyed mystification and genuine respect for the absurdity of his enterprise. Perhaps in a day when Camus and others have recognized the positive significance of the absurd in human existence, the basic foolishness of preaching evidenced in the missionary movement continues to give it symbolic power in the Western world. The cartoons of missionaries that continually appear in *The New Yorker* and similar sophisticated magazines would seem to substantiate this statement. They are often critical and even caustic caricatures, but they are often, at the same time, evident signs of the continuing symbolic mystification that foreign missionary work exerts on the popular mind precisely because of its essential absurdity and unintelligibility.

Modern man is hungry for such living symbols. As David Daiches says: "For a long time literature depended on heroes, but in our time it has had to learn to live without them." His explanation for this is that: "Prudence and knowledge are the enemies of heroism, and the hero in modern literature has succumbed to a series of attacks, first by the former and then by the latter. Too intimate a knowledge of a hero inevitably reduces his stature. No man is a hero to his valet—or to his psychoanalyst. . . . Knowledge thus dissolves value in explanation and substitutes inevitable loneliness for communion. The dissolution of value makes heroic stature impossible; but what about loneliness?"[1]

The increased knowledge of the world made possible by improved communications and means of travel has made the "exotic" world of the foreign missionary familiar to everyone. This has partly destroyed his unintelligibility and thus his symbolic power. Also the tremendous increase of international personnel exchange through commercial, military, and political agencies has made the mere fact of working in a foreign land commonplace. This has also served to "demystify" the foreign missionary movement and thus reduce its symbolic impact.

Ironically, however, the foreign missionary enterprise itself has done most to destroy its own symbolic powers, and that in two ways:

In the first place, the missionary movement became increasingly institutionalized. Itself a protest against the conservative, unimaginative, and self-sufficient ecclesiastical establishments, eventually it too became an establishment. Absurd and unintelligible in its visionary origins, it gradually became prudential and knowledgeable in its operations. Pioneering adventures started with about 13 pounds, such as the Baptist Missionary Society founded by Carey and his "consecrated cobblers," became the big business of American mission boards one of which, for example, has a $34,000,000 yearly budget.

The implications of this organizational rationalization do not need to be spelled out. Thirteen English pounds collected in a snuff box is an absurd beginning to the conversion of India. Thirty-four million dollars administered from a New York skyscraper begins to make sense, even to the most calloused materialistic mind. Thus, through a highly organized, highly efficient, highly promoted missionary enterprise, the symbol loses its grip.

The very magnitude of the enterprise and the large scale of its program encourages not only bureaucratic mentality among its managers but, most dangerous of all, encourages a spirit of prudence among its strategists. As David Daiches says, "as for prudence, that is always the ultimate destroyer of a heroic age." But, like the novelists, so the missionary propagandists and public relations experts "even found ways of making prudence heroic." However, though it is possible through the skillfulness of communication gymnastics that "he may remain *interesting* (indeed, he will gain a new kind of interest) . . . he loses stature.[2]

The new missionary symbols are not the low-born, low-bred mechanics in Serampore but the high-pressure, highly trained mechanics in New York or London, the organization men able to turn out a magnificently balanced budget and to rationalize their statistics skillfully on an I.B.M. machine. The symbol loses its grip.

If prudence and knowledge are to be the ultimate criteria for the missionary movement, we may cite the words of one who exhibits these qualities in their finest form and who has the additional advantage of viewing the situation with some objectivity. In an article entitled "As the Missionary's Era Ends," C. L. Sulzberger, publisher of *The New York Times*, writes from Mbarara, Uganda:

Historically speaking, the age of the missionary is draw-to a close. That is why so many brave, self-sacrificing Christian churchmen are experiencing troubles in Africa and Asia. In the collective mind of new Afro-Asian nations, the white missionary is associated with white colonialism.

Today there are missionary difficulties in Burma among the Karens, India among the Nagas, South Sudan among the Dinkas; in the Congo, Rwanda, and elsewhere. For reasons wholly unintended by the courageous men and women who devote themselves to instructing and caring for backward peoples, missionaries encounter opposition and new dangers. Following decolonialization there is pressure for demissionarization.

In this capital of a subkingdom in Uganda, an Anglican bishop assigned to Rwanda has been waiting for a visa he almost certainly won't receive. Missionaries have been savagely butchered in the Congo and expelled from feverish South Sudan. Even in this country's relative calm they face potential embarrassment.

Milton Obote, Ugandan Prime Minister, observes: "We could have trouble here. One thing missionaries don't realize is the need for separating church and state. They often want a say in government decisions and sometimes they openly support election candidates. People then imagine church conspiracies and, since most missionaries are white, they suspect them of working for a foreign country. We don't even like the word 'missionary.' We would avoid difficulties by having more African clergymen; after all, churches are international. White missionaries have done good work, but their era is finished."

Missionaries have become unwittingly entangled in burgeoning political movements and, because of their skin pigmentation, cannot escape becoming symbols. Take the case of South Sudan, from which they are being expelled. The Negroid South Sudanese tribes are ruled by northern Arab Moslems. The primitive southern Dinka tribesmen received what education they possess from missionaries. When students in Juba struck after an Arab instructor called one of them a slave, they were charged with subversion. The missionaries back them, as they have also backed oppressed minorities in the Burmese and Indian hills. This is abstract justice but concrete politics.

Obote charges the political organization inspiring Sudanese refugee activities here is the South Sudan Christian organization. President Kayibanda of Rwanda claims funds raised by missionary groups to aid emigrant Tutsi tribesmen are being used to arm not feed them.

By both proselytizing and educating, the missionaries cannot avoid political involvement. In Rwanda they impartially educate children of the Tutsi minority and Jutu majority. They find the Tutsis better pupils; therefore the Tutsis get better instruction and better jobs. When the Jutus persecuted the Tutsis, many missionaries sought to protect the latter and earned official condemnation.

Missionaries are caught in inter-religious rivalry between Catholic- and Protestant-educated politicians, while both sects in the Sudan see an Islamic plot to oust them. And racism obtrudes in the Congo, where white missionaries stand out as easy targets for atavistic cruelty.

Responsible non-Christian leaders naturally abhor such persecutions. The late Sheikh Shaltout, rector of Cairo's Al Azhar Theological Seminary and leading religious figure in

Islam, told me last October, for example, that he had no use for the black Muslim aberration in the U.S.A., because it preaches racism, and Islam ignores man's color.

In 1875 Stanley, the explorer-journalist, wrote: "Oh that some pious, practical missionary would come here. . . . Such a one if he can be found would become the savior of Africa." The missionaries did come and they did a remarkable civilizing job. They left a visible impact just as colonialism, for all its demerits, left a visible impact.

But the new nations want to run their own churches and they want missionary institutions like schools, but they want them turned over as rapidly as possible to their own clergymen. As with colonialism, they want the products of missionaries and the generosity of their sponsors; they don't want colonialists or missionaries themselves.[3]

These observations by a widely traveled, highly intelligent, and well-informed commentator are as moving a tribute to the accomplishments of the missionary's movement and as perceptive an analysis of the present predicament facing that movement as can be found. They are also as fine a memorial to it as may ever be written. As an obituary, though, it applies to the end of the "missionary's era," which is something different from the end of the missionary era. According to prudence and knowledge, it is undeniable that the missionary enterprise, understood as belonging to the missionary, is finished if not completely gone. But as long as the church exists there will be a missionary era, for the mission belongs to the church and not to the missionaries.

Because of this mystery, missionaries may still have a place in Africa and elsewhere. According to prudence and knowledge their day is finished; but because the essential *raison d'être* of the missionary's vocation is symbolic, they may still have a place in the unintelligibility of God's hidden working. This statement should not be taken to mean that the form of the missionary enterprise from the missionary's era or the particular way in which the missionary's vocation is now embodied and expressed will be the same. It is doubtful that it could be. But it is unthinkable that the universal church, with its apostolic calling to the ends of the earth, will not always have those strangers and foreigners in all parts of the Lord's dominion who simply by their presence (in the French connotation) symbolically represent the apostolicity of the whole Body and what Jacques Ellul calls the "Presence of the Kingdom."

This is a different *raison d'être* than that traditionally given for the foreign missionary. In a letter to the editor of *The New York Times*, David M. Stowe, General Secretary of the Division of Overseas Ministries of the National Council of Churches, argues against the Sulzberger article that there is "substantial evidence that 'the missionary's era' is not at an end. Missionary dominance is ending, as it should; but missionary partnership has, I am convinced, a very promising future." He correctly points out that many Protestant bodies in Africa and Asia are "already independent of foreign control through the working out of a well-established missionary policy. All agencies related to the

91

National Council of Churches have long encouraged self-government, self-support and indigenous responsibility for evangelism and social welfare on the part of related churches overseas." He goes on: "Mr. Sulzberger speaks of the desire to have missionary institutions turned over to local churches. Again, this has been a settled policy of many mission boards for some years now. The chief inhibiting factor is the continuing need for foreign subsidy, with the inevitable sharing of effective control which it entails."[4]

But what image of the missionary does even this enlightened viewpoint project? It does, indeed, suggest that the modern foreign missionary symbolizes partnership. At the same time it reveals that the missionary continues to symbolize effective control—benevolent as it may be—by foreigners of these newly "independent" Christian bodies. Serious questions can be raised as to whether there is in fact a continuing need for foreign subsidy, for it may well be that the inner strength and vitality of a Christian community may be undermined more by outside financial and material subsidies than by the absence of such assistance. It is also questionable whether it is inevitable that such subsidies, when given, should entail the sharing of effective control. Bread cast upon the waters *must* be effectively controlled? As Roland Allen wisely says:

We fear it because we feel that it is something we cannot control. And that is true. . . . "The wind bloweth where it listeth," said Christ, and spontaneous activity is a movement of the Spirit in the individual and in the Church, and we cannot control the Spirit. . . . Teaching can be refused; control cannot be refused, if it is control; teaching leads to enlargement, control to restriction. To attempt to control spontaneous zeal is to attempt to restrict it; and he who restricts a thing is glad of a little but does not welcome much. Thus, many of our missionaries welcome spontaneous zeal, provided there is not too much of it for their restrictions. . . . Such missionaries pray for the wind of the Spirit but not for a rushing mighty wind. I am writing because I believe in a rushing mighty wind, and desire its presence at all costs to our restrictions. But if that is what we are talking about, it is futile to imagine that we can control it. Let us begin by acknowledging that we cannot. If we do that, we may escape from the confusion created by those who say that they have spontaneous expansion in their missions and welcome it and rejoice in it; and yet say also that they are sent to control and must control. By spontaneous expansion I mean something which we cannot control. And if we cannot control it, we ought, as I think, to rejoice that we cannot control it. For if we cannot control it, it is because it is too great not because it is too small for us. The great things of God are beyond our control. Therein lies a vast hope.[5]

If the prime test of the missionary's vocation is its symbolic effectiveness in illuminating the apostolicity of the whole church, does even the partner missionary —as long as he remains identified with effective control, however minimally—meet the test? Does he symbolize the free wind of the Spirit and spontaneous expansion, or does he represent foreign control and inhibited restriction? It is here that missionary policy and

93

practice have so often been schizophrenic. As Allen says:

Whether we consider our doctrine, or our civilization, or our morals, or our organization, in relation to a spontaneous expansion of the Church, we are seized with terror, terror lest spontaneous expansion should lead to disorder. We are quite ready to talk of self-supporting, self-extending and self-governing Churches in the abstract as ideals; but the moment that we think of ourselves as establishing self-supporting, self-governing Churches in the Biblical sense we are met by this fear, a terrible, deadly fear. . . . We instinctively think of something which we cannot control as tending to disorder.[6]

"The chief inhibiting factor . . . [is] the inevitable sharing of effective control." This restrictive mentality arises from a misconception of the missionary's vocation: from thinking of him as a missionary agent rather than as an apostolic symbol.

The missionary movement itself has played an important role in destroying its own symbolic powers by its vocational individualism. Just as its institutionalization has obscured the mystery of the foolishness of preaching as God's wisdom of salvation and rationalized away the symbolic power of communal Christian witness, so by its misconception of missionary vocation in individualistic terms it also has undermined the symbolic power of individual missionary service.

Reinhold Niebuhr writes:

The attempt to maintain an absolute Christian ethic

against the relativities of politics, essentially the strategy of the Christian ascetic, is a valuable contribution to Christian thought and life. We ought to have not only the symbol of the Cross, but recurring historical symbols of the tension between the Christian ideal and the relativities and compromises in which we are all involved. The missionary movement has provided Protestantism with the only symbol of this kind at all comparable to the ascetic movement in Catholicism.[7]

On one side, the symbolic value of the missionary's vocation has been undercut by the tendency to consider it the apex of a vocational hierarchy. The calling of one Christian to serve, possibly abroad, as a missionary has symbolic significance for the whole community only insofar as the apostolicity of all believers is acknowledged. That is, the foreign missionary articulates and embodies the missionary-apostolic nature of the church as a whole. The apostolicity of the church is denied when missionary vocation becomes, to paraphrase an old ditty, "a vehicle built for few."

On the other side, the symbolic value of the missionary's vocation has been broken down by the institutional pressures which demand empirical and statistical evidence of success. Paul D. Clasper, a Baptist missionary who has served in Burma, has applied some of the insights of William Whyte's *The Organization Man* to the foreign mission enterprise and drawn some provocative conclusions. He says: "The conclusion would seem to be inescapable that a great share of the problems with which the missionary wrestles, and which he sometimes thinks are peculiarly his because he is a missionary, are really the common concerns of all organization men." And he goes on to suggest that not only does this institutional pressure lead to the absolutization of mediocrity as the standard which determines the selection of foreign missionary candidates—"the one most likely to maintain the team spirit and best fit into The Organization"—(he wonders if either St. Paul or William Carey would pass) but the constant pressure to "produce" is corrosive to morale, to creativity, and to spontaneous imaginative initiative.[8]

The vocational myth, then, has done more than rob the church at large of its sense of missionary responsibility and an awareness of its essential nature as an apostolic community. It has also encumbered foreign missionaries themselves with illusions about the superiority of their vocation, as well as confused them about their particular, functional tasks "on the field," where it is evident that being a missionary is not in itself a sufficiently clear job description to guide anyone in his labors. As the head of a large Indonesian church commented when confronted with the offer of foreign "volunteers": "If they send us a 'missionary,' we won't know what to do with him. What we need is a professor in church history for the seminary." It may be that this is the reason that the term "evangelist," ironically, has become a euphemism used by some missionary magazines to describes the work of missionaries for whom no more concrete specification of their work can be found.

A book entitled *Church and Empire* (with a preface by the Archbishop of Canterbury) published in 1907 contains an essay "The Vocation of the Anglo-Saxon Race and England's Responsibility." The author, the Rev. Canon G. H. S. Walpole, says with disarming assurance:

England seems to be marked out by her position and history for the great work to which she is called. . . . England developed that marked strength of character which earned for her at once the dislike and admiration of other countries. Silent, reserved, insular as her people are, they have the advantage of their failings in the quiet strength, self-sufficiency, and independence which have proved of such untold value in their relations with subject races. Unlike the Jew and Roman in so many things, yet they have one main characteristic in common, that which their critics call pride and their friends personality. . . . With such singular gifts of Providence it might seem that there could be no serious danger threatening the vocation of the Anglo-Saxon people to take the lead in the evangelization of the world.

The identification of missionary vocation with a particular nation or ethnic group strikes us now, half a century later, as ludicrous. But will it appear any more bizarre in another fifty years than the identification commonly assumed today of missionary vocation with particular persons called foreign missionaries or with special agencies of the church called mission boards? Or, may not the idea of a whole nation or a people having a missionary vocation, pervertedly as that may be conceived, actually be closer to the truth that the

97

whole Christian community is involved in and engaged in mission than the idea that only certain members or certain parts of the church are truly missionary?

Can the mission of the church be symbolically revitalized? Is it possible for the church to resymbolize its apostolic character through other means than the foreign missionary movement itself if that movement (as seems likely) disappears?

One thing is clear: Until the old vocational myth is put aside, no new symbolization can take place. It is also equally clear that demythologizing must be followed by remythologizing. Man cannot live by bread alone. But the Word that gives him life more abundantly cannot be interpreted in the barren literalness which interprets missionary calling in terms of a vocational caste system, or which projects a missionary stereotype from the faded images of the eighteenth and nineteenth century missionary heroes. Nor can the remythologizing of the missionary enterprise be accomplished through the researches of scholars in dusty libraries, or by the frantic drafting of new apologias by ecumenical committees, or by bigger budgets.

Symbols are not thought out. They are lived out. This is the ever-new missionary challenge facing the church.

—A young Dutchman and his wife sit in a small cottage on an Indonesian island. They are the last remnants of a political empire. They are the last representatives of the Western missionary enterprise. They do nothing. They organize nothing. They run nothing. They are simply there. And the fact of their presence may be a more vivid symbol of the true meaning of Christian love, of the ultimate significance of the Christian mission, to Christians and non-Christians alike, than all the "Christian civilization" and "Christian evangelization" with which nationals have been forcibly confronted for the previous three centuries.

—An English bishop in India leaves the mission field to which he had offered his life and devotion, to return to the West as an ecclesiastical bureaucrat and ordinary strap-hanging commuter so that his Indian colleagues can assume their responsibilities as leaders of their church. His leaving more than his coming symbolizes to many the meaning of Christian apostolate.

—The bishop of an Indonesian church, prematurely greyed by years of revolution and social and economic turmoil, turns down offers to go abroad for study or work in order that he may continue the thankless job of tending the flock, his mission.

—Not counting the cost, a gifted professional illustrator devotes his artistic talents and imaginative craftsmanship to the service of an ecumenical agency. His drawings and designs and photographs literally symbolize the worldwide *oikumene*.

—A Congregational minister with the warmth of human friendship and rare pastoral intuition forms a unique personal bridge between the church and the alienated worlds of culture and the arts in the intellectual milieu of New York City. The foolishness of preaching is accented, for his work is done without words—with little appreciation or financial support.

99

—A West Indian pastor, former legal assistant, ecumenical administrator, evangelist in backwoods Haiti, serves an English missionary society as a board secretary and symbolizes the missionary interdependence of the new ecumenical era.

—A Chinese priest leaves the West to return to the revolutionary ambiguities of his homeland, becoming a bishop and theological professor, a new-style missionary martyr whose natural identification with his field camouflages the intrinsic alienation from both East and West of those who proclaim the Word.

—An Episcopal lawyer, newly out of Harvard, immerses himself in the shadowy streets of Harlem and so identifies himself with its voiceless oppressed that his spoken and written polemics become one of their strong weapons in dispersing their darkness.

—The dean of a theological school loses his position because his championing of the rights of a minority group student alienates the academic principalities and ecclesiastical powers.

—An African doctor, trained in North America, puts aside his sterile surgeon's mask and spotless antiseptic gloves and enters the turbulent, "contaminated" arena of politics to become a cabinet minister in his new nation's government—as an act of Christian vocation.

—Each afternoon at three-thirty, at the corner of Broadway and 122nd Street, between the adjacent Union and Jewish Theological Seminaries, a car pulls up and three Protestant divinity students and three Jewish get in to ride to Washington. Arriving there, they go to the Roman Catholic Church of the Holy Comforter, which is located in a predominantly Negro neighborhood of the city. A Roman Catholic divinity student joins one Protestant and one Jewish student, and they drive to the Lincoln memorial, where the three get out and stand in silence for a few hours, until another three students, one from each faith, arrive to replace them. This informal organization, the Theological Students' Vigil for Civil Rights, maintained an around-the-clock vigil from April 19th until the civil rights bill was passed. Their plan was to continue the vigil, signs carried by the participants put it, "Night and Day as a Witness to Our Common Effort to Help Secure Justice and Equal Rights for All Our Citizens by Passing the Civil Rights Bill as It Came from the House."

One ten-year-old Negro boy, carefully reading the signs, was asked by a white companion what they said. "Man," said he, "They're all saying the exact same thing."

True apostolic signs always say the exact same thing.

5 THE ECUMENICAL REALITY

I have never seen anyone die for the ontological argument. . . . Whether the earth or the sun revolves around the other is a matter of profound indifference. . . . Solely the balance between evidence and lyricism can allow us to achieve simultaneously emotion and lucidity.

Albert Camus, *The Myth of Sisyphus*

MARCUS AURELIUS ONCE COMMENTED THAT THE ORIGIN OF great changes is simply "looking at things from a different angle." This is already evident in the missionary enterprise. The dawn of the ecumenical era has meant that many things are viewed from a new perspective, and not least the mission of the church. This new view, however, has disclosed more of the defects and limitations of the old order than it has provided a vision of what the new might be. James B. Conant, former president of Harvard University, in describing the changing scientific scene from 1900-1950, and in particular the contradictory wave and corpuscular theories of light, says that "what has happened in the last forty years is that physicists have learned to love a situation they once thought to be intolerable."[1]

An analogy might be drawn to the missionary movement in the present century. On the one hand, the traditional *raison d'être* of missions had a simplicity and inner coherence which made it easily communicable. It was understandable at the popular level, and the "ordinary" church member could identify himself with it in a simple and unambiguous way. The tremendous record of grass roots support for foreign missions in the last century and a half testifies to this fact. Furthermore, the simplicity of the traditional call to mission had an undoubted power of touching the deepest levels of Christian vocational response. The record of missionary service again speaks for itself:

Never . . . has any movement of any kind, political, religious, or otherwise, been supported by the voluntary gifts of so many individuals scattered in so many different lands. . . . The missionary movement of the past century has been the most notable outpouring of life, in the main unselfish, in the service of alien peoples which the world has ever seen."[2]

On the other hand, this simplistic *raison d'être*, epitomized by the old slogan of the Student Volunteer Movement, "The Evangelization of the World in This Generation," provided an inadequate ideological and theological undergirding for the movement and did not provide the conceptual categories necessary to deal with the increasing organizational and strategic problems posed by the gradual process of institutionalization of the missionary enterprise. A recent article on the role of slogans points out that psychologists say that "to be fully effective a slogan should express a single idea in seven words or less." Precisely because of this compression, however, which is one secret of their evocative power, slogans tend to "compress a lot of truth into what is basically an untruth," as Dean George Mowry of The University of California at Los Angeles puts it.[3] The oversimplification of the problem of the relation between church and world, which the traditional understanding of missions incorporated and on which it was mythologically based, presupposed a radical discontinuity between church and world in God's redemptive activity. It implied, too, that the plan of salvation was a process of conversion of individuals from the world into the Church by means of evangelization, a process in which missions was the preeminent Christian responsibility. It involved a "flat" dimensional perspective of the missionary frontiers (the geographical myth), a falsified view of the relation between the Christian way of life and non-Christian cultures (the cultural myth), an evolutionary and voluntaristic doctrine of the church (the ecclesiological myth), and a hierarchial idea of Christian vocation with foreign missionary service at the apex (the vocational myth).

This whole mythological complex, what we generally

term "missions," is sharply challenged by the ecumenical revolution. As Bishop Lesslie Newbigin points out in *The Household of God,* the ecumenical movement can never be understood if it is not approached from its beginnings in the missionary movement and will become fatally corrupted if it is untrue to its missionary origins. Or as he writes in *The Reunion of the Church:* "The missionary movement of the last two hundred years was a slow, painful and often reluctant obedience of the Churches of the West to the fundamental demand of the Gospel." Magnificent as this response has been, and heroic as its achievements undoubtedly are, the ecumenical movement itself presents a story of reluctant obedience of the churches not only of the West but of the whole world "to the fundamental demand of the Gospel," which may prove in retrospect to be equally magnificent and heroic. The paradoxical polarity of the missionary enterprise and the ecumenical movement lies in the fact that the miraculous birth of ecumenical consciousness within the Christian global community has, among other things, made it clear that the classical missions response of the churches is not the only, or even the most adequate, obedience to the demand of the gospel. The missionary enterprise is not, at least in its traditional form, the ultimate means of gospel obedience. In short, the ecumenical movement has raised radical questions about what the fundamental demand of the gospel actually is.

It might be added, therefore, that the missionary movement will become fatally corrupted if it is not true to its ecumenical fulfilment. This dialectical relation is explicated in the complementary yet contradictory connection between mission and unity. At the International Missionary Council meeting at Willingen in 1952 it was affirmed:

The love of God in Christ calls for the three fold response of worship, unity and mission. These three aspects of the Church's response are interdependent; they become corrupted when isolated from each other. Division in the Church distorts its witness, frustrates its mission, and contradicts its own nature. If the Church is to demonstrate the Gospel in its life as well as in its preaching, it must manifest to the world the power of God to break down all barriers and to establish the Church's unity in Christ. Christ is not divided.

In other words, the demand of the gospel not only requires *both* the response of mission and unity: the ecumenical movement represents the reluctant obedience of the churches to the fact that the denial of either, or the failure to maintain the dual demand in polar tension, means a negation of both.

Looked at historically, the nineteenth century might be thought of as the missionary century, in which the imperative to carry the gospel to the world was gradually recognized as implicit in the nature of the gospel itself. The twentieth century, as the ecumenical century, has seen the gradual recognition that also implicit in the gospel is the imperative of Christian unity. Furthermore, it has gradually dawned on the Christian community that the credence of the world to the proclamation of Christ depends on the visible manifestation of unity by Christ's people: *ut omnes unum sint . . . ut credat mundus.*

The credibility of the good news that Christ has been sent by God can be assured only by the oneness of those who believe. In their unity the divine unity of Father and Son is reflected, and their unity verifies the love that Christ embodies and God intends for the world. The church as the fellowship of believers incorporates the "sentness," the mission, of Christ to the world: it is, as the Body of Christ, God's mission to and in the world. Insofar as it fails by disunity to manifest its essential nature, it is disobedient to its missionary calling. Mission, therefore, is not something added on to the church but something that belongs to its fundamental character. And unity is not something the church can work out, or develop, in order to facilitate its missionary effectiveness. Insofar as the church does not exhibit its unity it is not missionary at all, for it denies its own God-given nature as the corporate extension of God's mission to the world in Christ.

In one sense, this dialectical polarity of unity and mission, a truth whose full recovery is partially dependent on the yet-incomplete merging of the missionary movement of the nineteenth and the ecumenical movement of the twentieth century, is simply descriptive of the inner dynamic of the church. In previous periods of church history, ecclesiological debate centered around the formal constitution of the church. The classical Christian confessions have approached the doctrine of the church in this external, institutional way, and the relation of mission and unity has generally been interpreted in such formal categories. The ecclesiological revolution arising out of the missionary and ecumenical movements derives in part from the fact that the church is coming to be understood in dynamic rather than formal terms. Just as in the atomic era physicists are dealing with matter as energy, so ecclesiologically the church is seen in the ecumenical era to be a reality that can be described not only in formal terms but also, and perhaps more adequately, in dynamic and "energetic" categories. An understanding of the church as a living organism incorporating unity and mission is the result of the rediscovery of the nature of the church through the missionary and ecumenical movements.

This dynamic ecclesiology explicates certain paradoxical aspects of church history that have resisted rational analysis on the basis of the older, formal ecclesiologies. It has often been an embarrassment to Christian chroniclers that the periods of missionary initiative have tended to coincide with those of divisiveness and sectarianism in the life of the church. Christian expansion seems to be realized only at the expense of the unity of the church. Or, to look at it from the other side, church unity seems to be most manifestly exhibited at times of missionary dormancy, or to be achieved mainly by either suppression or exclusion of dynamic revivalist movements with their explosive, expansionist characteristics. Depending on the biases of the interpreters, such phenomena have been explained largely as results of sin—either those of the movements or individuals whose expansionist traits threatened the unity of the church, or those of persons whose efforts to maintain the unity of the church threatened expansionist missionary endeavors. The "bad guys" and the "good guys" of church history are thus likely to be identified in accordance with the particular bias of the historian (and to some extent that of the tradition he represents, consciously or unconsciously). That is, the relative importance a particular historian attaches to mission and unity as essential attributes of the church will determine which are "good" or "bad." Since most church history, until relatively modern times at least, has been written by representatives of the ecclesiastical establishments, it has been almost inevitable that their records have a "church-type" outlook (to use Troeltsch's typology). As a result, "sect-type" missionary phenomena have generally been treated negatively, by being either dismissed as heretical or simply ignored. For the same reason, the dynamic polarity of mission and unity as a clue to the vitality of the Christian community has almost entirely been lost.

A more ecumenically oriented church history may reveal that the life of the church depends on this polar tension between mission and unity and that the degree to which this tension is maintained, rather than resolved, determines the health of the ecclesiastical body. The church-type historian is inclined to view church history as a series of declines and reforms, in which the unity of the church is always precariously maintained in the face of expansionist, and thus divisive, pressures. The sect-type historian, on the other hand, is inclined to see Christian history as a tide of missionary expansion, whose advance is constantly being checked by recessive forces of ecclesiastical introversion or consolidation. A more ecumenical historical perspective seems to show that the tension between mission and unity has been evident in every era and in all types of Christian communities and that, in fact, the existence of this unresolved tension is the clue to the creativity and liveliness of the church through the ages. When the tension is relaxed, vitality diminishes: unity realized at the expense of missionary outreach results in introverted stagnation, and mission realized at the expense of unity results in fragmentary dissolution.

As has been suggested, this historical dialectic is a reflection of the essential theological reality of the church as well as of its inescapable relation with the world. The first major threat to the unity of the church was posed by missionary expansion. The Jerusalem Council, whose turbulent deliberations are recorded in the Acts of the Apostles, was struggling to maintain Christian unity in the face of expansionist pressures. Apostolic missionary outreach not only strained the territorial lines of unity identified with the original Jerusalem fellowship, but the success of apostolic preaching among non-Jewish people meant that the unity of the church based on, or coincidental with, the ethnic homogeneity of the primitive fellowship of Jewish disciples had to be radically questioned and reexamined. The achievement of the Jerusalem Council was that through it the church moved beyond a static conception of unity to a dynamic one. In other words, if the unity of the church was to be maintained it had to have a form sufficiently comprehensive and flexible to encompass the full reality of the Body as living, expanding, and changing.

This has meant that throughout history the church has constantly had to change the form of its unity to meet the demands imposed by its ecumenical nature and charter. Whenever it has failed to do so, schism and dissolution have resulted. The Protestant Reformation, for example, could be so interpreted. The form of unity of medieval Catholicism was inadequate to cope with the ecumenical expansion of the church; the old form of unity, centered in Rome and largely oriented toward southern European Christianity, was increasingly strained and finally broken by the new Christian concentrations in the north and west—the results of the church's own missionary efforts. Indeed, one might say that Vatican Council II is a belated, though energetic, attempt of the Roman Catholic Church to find a new form of unity to do justice not only to the ecumenical expansion of Christianity in its "separated" Orthodox and Protestant expressions but also to the ecumenical extension of the Roman communion itself throughout the inhabited earth since medieval times. In short, any form of Christian unity that is not truly ecumenical is by definition not true unity. Any form of Christian unity that does not provide possibilities of missionary expansion, or adequately incorporate the results of that expansion, is inevitably shattered.

The arduous struggle to work out the relation between unity and mission, and the search for a new understanding of the connection between church and world, has not led to frustration for those engaged in this ecumenical intellectual endeavor but it has been an experience through which they "have learned to love a situation they once thought to be intolerable." The realization has gradually, in some ways too slowly, dawned that this polar tension between unity and mission, between the cohesive and expansive characters of the gospel, between the church and the world, rather than being an intolerable contradiction is the dialectical basis for a new dynamic concept of the missionary task. Thus, the ecumenical transformation, though it may spell the end of one era of mission, even more promises the beginning of a new one—more profound, more comprehensive, more vital than the one it succeeds.

The ecumenical transformation is based on the recovery of two fundamental biblical insights. The first is the reality that *the mission field is the world*. Jesus said simply: "the field is the world." (Matt. 13:38) The end of God's love is the world and his whole plan of salvation is directed toward it: he "so loved *the world* that he gave his only Son." And this is the basis of mission, for missionary vocation is based on God's mission, which is for the world. "God sent the Son into the world, not to condemn the world, but that the world might be saved through him."

Christians are those in the world who have accepted God's love, not for themselves in themselves, but as representatives of the world that God intends to save. The world not only gives meaning to the existence of Christians, but it also defines and determines the nature and purpose of their mission. Thus, Christians are called to turn toward the world. They are, as it were, persons sent to and into the world, to "turn their backs on God."

The missionary frontier is found wherever the world is confronted with God's love. The missionary frontier is, therefore, multidimensional. The various geographical frontiers are real missionary frontiers because it is the whole world that God loves, and this gospel must be proclaimed to the ends of the earth. God's love, however, includes more than the horizontal dimensions of the world's existence. The geographical frontier symbolizes all those frontiers of the world that the gospel confronts and crosses over—sociological, cultural, political, intellectual. The Christian mission, as an expression of God's mission, means not only going *out to* but also *into* the world. As Paul writes to the Romans: "For I am sure that neither death, nor things present, nor things to come, nor powers, nor height, nor depth, nor anything else in all creation, will be able to separate us from the love of God in Christ Jesus our Lord."

There is inevitably a foreignness in the missionary enterprise, but that foreign character has not in the

113

first instance anything to do with geographical categories. Geography may for some be a reason for their separation from the love of God in Christ. It is, nevertheless, only one gulf that God's mission leaps over. An unexplored tract of jungle in New Guinea may be a foreign frontier of the mission; but so is the new urban megalopolis. Or the intellectual enclaves of a great university. Or the racial ghettoes of a modern society.

The Report of a World Council of Churches study commission on "Theological Reflections on the Missionary Task of the Church" puts it this way:

1) There is one Gospel, and it requires faithful witness to all men, to the ends of the earth. The task is one, and its pursuance is always a necessary part of the Church's obedience to God. Every frontier, of whatever kind, has to be crossed in the fulfilling of this commission.

2) The term "nation" is used in sufficiently broad ways in the Bible to warrant its application to peoples in their total linguistic, social, cultural and religious settings. The witness of the Gospel must be made to men as they actually are, within the groupings of nation, community, occupation, culture and religion in which they actually live. The whole structure of meanings found in such groupings is an inseparable part of the lives of those who live and work within them, and must be taken with full seriousness in the missionary task. It must be recognized, moreover, that these groupings and settings are always subject to change, and that witness to the Gospel must also take account of this.

3) Neither sociological nor geographical boundaries are of ultimate theological significance for the mission of the

People of God, since Christ has broken down the walls which separate men and groups from one another, and is fashioning one new humanity. It is, however, important for the Church accurately to identify those boundaries which empirically separate men from each other, since only so can the strategy of its missionary task be effectively directed.[3]

The ecumenical transformation is also based on the recovery of a second fundamental biblical insight: *the church is the mission.* There is only one gospel for the one world, and there is only one church to bear witness to that reality. As has been suggested, the expansive nature of the church is rooted in the character of God's love, which is meant for the whole world in every dimension of its existence. The cohesive character of the church is similarly rooted in the love of God. God's love is outgoing: it sends those whom it reaches and transforms. God's love, however, not only sends out; it sends together. Every missionary, therefore, as one who is a sign of God's love, must symbolize both the expansive nature of that love and its cohesive character. The missionary must represent *both* the mission and the unity of the church, because only then is he an adequate sign of the fullness of God's love.

On one hand, therefore, this means that the love of God constrains the church to manifest the cohesive nature of love in its inner life. The whole Body, as the corporate embodiment of the love of God, must manifest the essential unity of God himself. The relation between the various parts of the Body must reflect this ultimate divine oneness, and more particularly the divine unity of the Father and the Son—"one, even as we are one." Ecclesiastical interchurch relationships always stand to be measured by this final theological criterion. Christian fragmentation must be judged not on the basis of some functional criterion such as efficiency, but on the basis that church disunity is an ontological denial of God's unitary being, which the church should symbolize in the world and to the world.

On the other hand, to confess that the church is the mission means that a harmonic relationship between the parts of the Body can never be an end in itself. Christian unity cannot be introverted. That would also be an ontological denial of God's being. The end of God's love is not the church, it is the world. One might say that God only loves the church because it *is* the world—the world that recognizes and confesses and reflects his love for the whole of creation. Some forms of unity can be false because they are introverted—that is, when unity is realized at the expense of mission and thereby denies the fullness of God's love, which is both centripetal and centrifugal, and ignores the final goal of his love, which is the world. As Colin Williams points out in *Where In The World?* there is justification, in this context, of speaking of "heretical structures"; he reports the conclusion of the Western European Working Group of the WCC Study on "The Missionary Stucture of the Congregation":

Heretical structures are structures which prevent the Gospel from reaching its intended goal. In other words, structures are heretical when they prevent the congregation from penetrating into every geographic and social realm, thus standing between the Gospel and the world.

One of the implications of this organic view of the church as mission is that every form of Christian confrontation with the world is seen to be authentically missionary. Whether this confrontation takes place in Calcutta or East Harlem, in West Java or East Oakland, in the Christian coffee house "Precarious Vision" in San Francisco or the Christian ashram in Jaffna, Ceylon, is, to use Camus' words, "a matter of profound indifference." There is from this standpoint no home and abroad, no foreign and domestic in the mission: it is simply the church in the world bringing the gospel to the world. The field is the world. Nothing more needs be said; nothing more can be said.

The second implication of the affirmation that the church is the mission is that not only must the whole church be structured to fulfill its missionary nature— the universal Body as well as the local congregation— but every member of the church must be a missionary. This need not deny the possibility of functional differentiation in the work of the various members, or a variety of workings of the members in expressing the variety of gifts of the Holy Spirit in the Body. The term "missionary," however, may be used for specific members only insofar as it is understood to represent the mission of the whole Body and to symbolize the fact that a missionary is commissioned by the Body as a whole to signify its missionary nature.

To look at the Christian mission from this ecclesiological and global perspective does not invalidate foreign missions in the traditional sense, or exclude foreign missionary as a meaningful vocational category. From this ecumenical viewpoint, however, it is evident that the church, in moving from one land to another or in sending representatives to the ends of the earth, is not doing something extraordinary but rather something that is perfectly normal. For if the field is the world and the church is the mission, why should Christians *not* go everywhere? And the question for the Christian is not: "Should I be a missionary?" or "Why should I go?" The right question is: "Being a missionary, why should I *not* go?" Ecumenically considered, the question of where is "a matter of profound indifference"; there is no need for proof or a special calling to go from New York to Tokyo (or vice versa) or from Fifth Avenue to East Harlem (or vice versa). For the Christian this foreign movement, strange and extraordinary as it may appear to the outsider, is the natural expression of the nature of the gospel and the ordinary symbol of God's intention for the world. The burden of proof, in short, is not on those who go but on those who fail to go.

The ecumenical understanding of the church as mission also means that the distinction between clergy and laity must be radically reappraised. It is theologically evident that the mission of the church cannot be identified either with religious specialists (missionaries) or with particular religious institutions (mission boards).

118

But even on functional grounds there are reasons for suspecting this kind of traditional categorization of the specialized vocations within the Body. A new missionary vision is emerging to replace it. Gibson Winter writes:

The servant Church emerges as a community of highly sensitive and theologically self-conscious laymen. . . . The laity can no longer relegate the apostolate to religious specialists. They bear the burden of discerning the meaning of events in the human struggle. The crucial role of the Church in a secularized world only becomes clear as it is seen in the servanthood of the laity in that world.[4]

The organizational ramifications of an ecumenically transformed view of mission are many, and they are only beginning to be tentatively envisioned. For one thing, the pattern of the future, as far as we can understand it, would appear to have little place for traditional organizational patterns of missions. Mission boards, if they exist at all, will evidently have to serve other functions in relation to the church's mission than they have served in the past. This, of course, has already happened to some extent: modern mission boards tend to be the liaison agencies for the churches' international ecclesiastical relations. They are in many cases more like foreign affairs offices of the churches than mission boards in the classical sense. In the future, however, this transformation may be even more radical. It may be, for instance, that instead of recruiting missionaries or supporting and managing mission institutions the mission board of the future may be much more engaged in training laymen to fulfill a missionary vocation in a secular occupation or, on the other hand, in being an ecumenical clearing house, receiving requests for specialized types of service from other churches and calling upon those within their own body who have the qualifications to meet these needs. Far from restricting their missionary responsibility, this would actually enlarge the role of such boards, for presumably they would be expected to look on the total manpower resources of the Christian community in meeting missionary demands instead of having to depend only on those who, for one reason or another, have volunteered as missionary prospects.

Beyond moving more into the sphere of ecumenical interchurch aid and personnel exchange, the mission board of the future might also be expected to be less engaged in recruiting and managing its own missionary corps and more involved in training and educating lay missionaries for service in secular organizations both at home and abroad. In part this would mean educating the whole laity to its missionary obligations. But it would also mean preparing people for more specialized types of service, especially those with peculiarly strategic missionary potentiality. The spectacular development of the Peace Corps vividly illustrates the change in the international scene which, on the one hand, has made certain aspects of the missionary work of the churches anachronistic and, on the other hand, has presented the churches with unparalleled opportunities for missionary penetration into worlds that have been closed to the gospel because of the gospel's association in the past with institutional Christianity. As the WCC Commission on the Missionary Task of the Church reported:

Those who believe themselves to be missionaries have increasing opportunities to go to other countries, in a variety of occupations, without being directly related to mission agencies. The Church should clearly recognize the validity and importance of this type of missionary call. Where, in particular instances, the Christian community feels able to confirm the reality of this vocation, the church from which such a missionary comes, and the church to which he or she goes, should be prepared to encourage and assist the fulfillment of this vocation.

It should be further noted that, in a world in which new social groupings are constantly forming, and in which Christians are moving about in their secular occupations as never before, the possibilities of lay witness constitute the Church's greatest opportunity to penetrate new areas with the Gospel. It is essential that laymen should be helped to recognize this fact and to accept the full implications of their baptism. The churches must develop ways of preparing them for effective participation in the one mission.

Camus said: "I have never seen anyone die for the ontological argument." Camus would probably expect martyrdom even less for the ecclesiological argument. He would be right, but only partly. For men and women have, in fact, died for the church. For the church, however, and not for arguments about it. Or perhaps more accurately, the martyrs have given themselves willingly to the world, through the church, for the love of Christ.

The ecumenical argument is a necessary preparation for mission, for it offers a new perspective on the relation of the church and the world, which is more profound and more comprehensive than the old mythology of missions. Nevertheless, the ecumenical argument, however much more adequately it describes the nature and dimensions of the missionary task facing the church today than does the old mythology, has yet to prove its ability to evoke the same passionate vocational response from the Christian community that the old missionary message drew out.

Can it? No. It cannot. Moreover, it should not. Missionary dynamic is not generated by new theories. Nor is it created by breaking down old ones. Insofar as the ecumenical transformation has been brought about by a recovery of basic biblical truth about the nature of the world, the gospel, and the church, it may also bring a recovery of the meaning of Christian obedience and responsibility. Christian response is rooted in the deepest levels of spiritual existence, and its dynamic is drawn from the deepest sources of spiritual power. It is, therefore, not new missionary philosophies that will unleash the hidden forces of missionary passion in the Christian community, but a turning to God in praise and adoration and recognition as the Creator, Redeemer, and Sanctifier of all life. This will energize the Christian Body for mission. The Orthodox tradition, with its liturgical accent, has much to teach the whole church on the sources of Christian dynamic. Alexander Schmemann writes:

> . . . it is our certitude that in the ascension of the Church in Christ, in the Joy of the world to come, in the Church as the *sacrament*—the gift, the beginning, the presence, the promise, the reality, the anticipation—of the Kingdom, is the source and the beginning of all Christian mission. It is only as we return from the light and the joy of Christ's presence that we recover the world as a meaningful field of our Christian action, that we see the true reality of the world and thus discover what we must do.[5]

"The Spirit and the Bride say, 'Come'." When the Christian also learns to say "Come," he is ready to send. "Come, Lord Jesus! Come, Lord Jesus!" This eschatological cry, full of longing for that final healing of the brokenness and alienation of the world, is also the everyday liturgical chant of the Christian community, in individual prayer or in common worship. In this world, however, and in this time the Christian cannot remain in the sanctuary. The liturgy recalls him to God, but at the same time it recalls him to the world. He comes. He goes. But through the liturgy his going out into the world is not leaving. He goes out as one sent. His worship, his service, is within the church, to God; his worship, his service, is outside the church, to the world. The true worshiper, who worships in spirit and in truth, is also the true missionary. He worships in spirit—that is, he looks forward in hope to the resolution of all the ambiguities and paradoxes of human existence through the coming Christ. But he also worships in truth—that is, he recognizes in the earthly elements of the liturgy the reality of his actual existence in this world, to which Christ has come. In this tension between the glorious hope and the excruciating present that the liturgy epitomizes, the missionary response is inflamed. Worship ends in mission; mission ends in worship.

FOOTNOTES

INTRODUCTION

1. C. C. West and D. M. Paton (eds.), *The Missionary Church in East and West.* Naperville, Ill.: Allenson, 1959, p. 89.
2. Herbert Butterfield, *The Origins of Modern Science.* London: G. Bell, 1949.
3. *Catholic Voice,* October 1, 1964.
4. Butterfield, *Op. cit.*

CHAPTER 1

1. Joseph Conrad, "Youth," in *Typhoon and Other Tales.* New York: New American Library (Signet), 1963, p. 244.
2. J. H. Randall, *The Making of the Modern Mind.* Boston: Houghton Mifflin, 1940, p. 205.
3. *Ibid.,* p. 207.
4. *One Body, One Gospel, One World.* London: Carling, 1958, p. 12.

CHAPTER 2

1. Laurens van der Post, *Dark Eye in Africa.* New York: Morrow, 1955, pp. 20, 54-55.

2. H. W. Schneider in *Readings in the History of Mankind,* G. S. Metraux (ed.), Vol. 2, *The Nineteenth Century World.* New York: New American Library, pp. 337-338.

3. J. H. Bavinck, *The Impact of Christianity on the Non-Christian World.* Grand Rapids, Mich.: Eerdmans, 1948, pp. 27ff.

4. *Ibid.*

5. *Anatomy of Paradise.* New York: Sloane, 1948, p. 259ff.

6. W. D. Reyburn, "Identification in the Missionary Task." *Practical Anthropology,* January-February 1960, p. 10.

7. T. H. Easterfield, "Missions and Anthropology in the Solomons." *Frontier,* Vol. 1, No. 2, pp. 121-125.

8. *Upon the Earth.* New York: McGraw-Hill, 1962, p. 195ff.

9. "Towards an Indian Church," paper read at the Nagercoil Synod, 1958.

10. *Ibid.*

11. *Prisoner for God: Letters and Papers from Prison.* New York: Macmillan, 1954, p. 125.

12. *Ibid.,* p. 123.

13. *Ibid.,* p. 124.

14. "Search for Self-Identity: Asian People Today." *The Divinity School News,* University of Chicago, November 1, 1959, pp. 12-13.

15. *Frank Lloyd Wright: Writings and Buildings,* selected by Edgar Kaufmann and Ben Raeburn. New York: Horizon, p. 184.

16. Austin Farrer, *The Glass of Vision.* Westminster, England: Dacre, 1948, p. 45.

CHAPTER 3

1. *International Review of Missions,* October, 1957, p. 401ff.

2. Vol. 6, No. 3, p. 136.

3. M. Searle Bates, in *I.M.C. Survey of the Training of the Ministry in Africa.*

4. Paul Tillich, *The Protestant Era.* Chicago: U. of Chicago Press, 1948.

5. *Essays in Applied Christianity.* Cleveland: World (Meridian), p. 136.

6. *Pensées,* H. F. Stewart (ed.). New York: Cambridge University Press, p. 375.
7. "The Colour of Our Mammies." *Encounter,* July 1959.
8. Paul Tillich, *Op. cit.*

CHAPTER 4

1. Hiram Haydn and Betsy Saunders (eds.), *The American Scholar Reader.* New York: Atheneum, 1960, p. 379.
2. *Ibid.,* p. 380.
3. *The New York Times,* April 8, 1964.
4. *The New York Times,* April 9, 1964.
5. *The Spontaneous Expansion of the Church.* Grand Rapids, Mich.: Eerdmans, 1962, pp. 16, 17.
6. *Ibid.,* p. 18.
7. *An Interpretation of Christian Ethics.* New York: Harper, 1935, p. 187.
8. "The Denominational Missionary and the Organization Man." *Occasional Bulletin* of the Missionary Research Library, March 17, 1958.

CHAPTER 5

1. *Modern Science and Modern Man.* New York: Columbia U. Press, 1952, p. 70.
2. Kenneth Scott Latourette, *Missions Tomorrow.* New York: Harper, 1936, pp. 12, 15.
3. *Bulletin,* Division of Studies, World Council of Churches, Autumn 1961.
4. *The New Creation as Metropolis.* New York: Macmillan, 1963, pp. 63-64.
5. *For the Life of the World.* New York: National Student Christian Federation, 1963, pp. 85-86.

• BOOKNOTE •

Text Type: Linotype Caledonia
Display Type: Garamont
Manufacturer: Sowers Printing Company
Designer: Louise E. Jefferson

901   F.W.